Out of the Blue

VinnieCarla Agnello

Out of the Blue

A Suddenly Single Mother's Memoir of Love, Intuition, and Healing

Amore Press
New York, New York

Amore Press, LLC
119 West 72nd Street, #339
New York, New York 10023
www.amorepress.com

If you would like to do any of the above,
please contact reviews@*amore*press.com

For distribution, special sales to organizations, or licensing rights,
please contact sales@*amore*press.com

Cover, text design, and typography by Infinitum Limited.

ISBN: 978-0-9903365-0-1 (Print)

For Joey,
Salvatore, and Vincent

Contents

August 25, 2001

I OPENED MY EYES. MY PAJAMAS WERE WET AND STICKING TO my body. I could feel a rapid pulse pounding in my head, and my mouth was open gasping for air. I didn't know where I was at first, but with each breath I became aware. I could see the blurry outline of the side table. I reached out slowly and felt for my glasses then looked at the clock: 4:47 a.m.

Next to me baby Vincent was sleeping peacefully, and my son Sal, in his bed, was also fast asleep. I remembered that in the middle of the night I had gone to Vincent's bed to breast-feed him and had fallen asleep. I moved as slowly and as gracefully as one can with a racing heart and shaky limbs so as to not wake my sleeping sons.

I hurried to my bedroom. I had to know he was there. He had to be there, and then I caught sight of him—my husband—in our bed sleeping. A wave of relief came over me, but the feeling inside had not gone away. I was still shaking and my heart was still pounding. I quickly crawled under the covers and woke him and said, "Joey, please hold me. It was horrible." I needed to feel him and know that he was there. He was half awake, but he put his arms around me. I told him about my nightmare.

"There was this huge thing that happened. I think it was on a mountain. The military was involved, and so were a lot of people. I was not sure what had happened but I knew in my heart that you were part of it. I ran to find you. I was running and running and screaming your name, but I could not see where I was going because it was misty and full of white smoke. It was like I was running through a cloud, but it was hard to breathe. Time was going by and I kept calling out your name. For days and days I kept calling out to you, but as I got deeper and deeper into the smoke you seemed further away. I felt so alone and so sad, and I missed that I could not talk to you anymore. No one could find you. I started crying, and then I heard a voice in my head say that you were dead. I screamed and cried at the voice in my head, that I think was God, and begged that you were alive, but you were gone and it was so real."

I squeezed his arm and kissed him, smelling his scent, feeling his warmth. "Hold me tighter." I could feel the life that was in him, proving that it was only a dream.

"It's all right, I'm here," he said.

I wanted to believe him when he said it was just a dream. I lied to him and told him that he was right and that I felt better, but I knew that there was something different about this dream. It felt exactly like two dreams I'd had in the recent past, and both of those dreams had become a reality. I did not want to believe that this dream could become a reality. I would not allow it to be a premonition or occupy any more time in my mind.

I quickly focused on my reality: We were happily married with two toddlers, two dogs, and three cats. We both had careers we loved, and we owned a house steps from the beach. In my head I repeated: My dream is not real, my life is real, and it is wonderful.

Life changes in the instant. The ordinary instant.
—Joan Didion, *The Year of Magical Thinking*

Part One

Suddenly Single

An Ordinary Day

SEPTEMBER 11, 2001

IT WAS FIVE THIRTY IN THE MORNING. I TRIED NOT TO MOVE, so I would not wake Vincent. In the middle of the night I had fallen asleep with him after he nursed. Morning had come too soon, and I was tired and trying not to breathe too hard for fear of waking him. Forty minutes earlier, I awoke to the sounds of Joey getting out of bed and the click-clacking of Chelsea and Durante's paws on the wooden floor trailing him. I heard the leashes and the door as they left for their morning walk. I had since fallen back to sleep and was reawakened by the front door opening and then the familiar sounds coming from the kitchen. I hoped that all the noise would not wake the boys. Sal was almost three and an early riser. It was only a matter of minutes until he would be awake and my rest would be over. I cringed as the electric can opener hummed. I looked over to Sal's bed, but he continued to sleep even as the ceramic dog bowls scraped across the floor as the dogs ate. The sound of Joey moving around the kitchen getting his breakfast grew louder. Please just give me a few more minutes. I closed my eyes making the most of my final moments of rest. I was starting to fall back to sleep when I heard Sal say, "Hi, Mommy." I whispered to him that his daddy was in the kitchen. I knew he would head straight for Joey. I was not ready to get out of bed and since Vincent was still sleeping, I could buy more time by sending Sal to his father.

"Hello, Salvatore," Joey said. This was bliss to my ears; I knew Joey would give Sal some of his cereal. Joey always put Sal on his lap, and he and Sal would take turns eating cereal from the same bowl. Joey would give Sal a spoonful of cereal and then he would take a spoonful. I could hear the two of them talking, and I enjoyed listening to them. I knew that I would not be able to go back to sleep, but I was content lying there not having to move. I knew by the clock that Joey would be calling me soon to say that he would have to leave for work. Joey's morning routine, when working a day shift at the firehouse, was always the same. He left at 6:15 a.m., so I relished the last few moments in bed enjoying the sounds and voices coming from the kitchen.

"Get up," he called. "I gotta go soon."

I would usually say, "I know, I know," but today was different, and showing no sign of my sleep deprivation or crankiness, I said sweetly, "I'll be right there." I got up without waking Vincent and I smiled as I entered the kitchen. The image of Sal and Joey sharing a bowl of cereal was one of my favorite sights. The dogs greeted me as Joey and Sal got up from the table. Sal began playing with his toys in the family room and Joey asked me about the schedule for the next day. I would be working and he wanted to know what time Sal had to be at his gymnastics class. He loved going to Sal's class because he and Vincent would jump on the trampoline and they had just as much fun as Sal.

As the minutes ticked away, Joey said he hoped Vincent would wake up so he could spend some time with him before he had to leave. Then as if on cue, Vincent called out, "Mommy." I went to him, quickly changing him so I could get him to the kitchen to see Joey. Vincent ran to him and Joey picked him up, hugging and kissing him. When he put him down, Vincent joined Sal, who was playing with blocks. As we watched the boys play, we smiled at each other hoping that Sal would not "accidentally" hit his brother with a block.

I hated that Joey had to go to work. I wished he could stay home and we could spend the day together, but I was happy knowing he did not have to work a twenty-four–hour shift and that he would be home for dinner. As he started to get his things together he asked me what we were having. I smiled. "Salmon with string beans and potatoes." Not many men want to know what's for dinner while still digesting breakfast, but Joey loved food and dinner was already on his mind. A good meal ranked high on his list of desires, almost equal to sex. We joked that the only person Joey would ever consider leaving me for was Lydia Bastianich, an older woman who had an Italian cooking show on PBS.

"Today is Tuesday." Joey spoke loudly so that Sal could hear him as he moved around the kitchen. "Salvatore has school today. He is such a big boy." Sal was turning three on the sixteenth, and he had just started his first day of nursery school on the previous Thursday. We loved being with the boys and did not really want to part with Sal but we knew that nursery school was important for his development, so we signed him up for two days a week.

That first morning of nursery school, Joey took Sal and stayed with him. Their bond was strong. Sal worshipped his dad, and Joey adored Sal. When possible, they were always together. If Joey was raking leaves, then Sal was right next to him raking leaves with a toy rake. When Joey would shave, Sal would shave with a fake razor that Joey had made for him. Sal admired that Joey was a firefighter and that he worked in construction as a part-time job. In Sal's toddler world there was only one thing as good as a firefighter and that was "Bob the Builder." Once when Sal and I were in our car stopped at a red light, he looked out the window at a very run-down house and announced, "My daddy could fix that. He would just need to get his ladder and his tools."

Whenever we were on a play date at someone's house and Sal did not want to leave his friend or the toys, all I had to say was "We have to go, because Daddy will be home soon," or "We're going to see Daddy," and Sal would drop whatever he was doing and rush to leave.

Before Joey left for work that morning, he walked to where the boys were playing and kissed and hugged each of them. I was standing at the kitchen entrance. Joey came toward me with a smile on his face. "Have fun," he said kissing me. "I love you."

He walked to the front door, turned and gazed back at me. We both smiled, and for a moment our eyes locked. Time slowed down, and what was probably just a few seconds I remember as minutes. A kind of intensity infused that moment, and it stirred something in my soul reminiscent of the very first time we met.

As powerful as it was—and as if it never happened—it ended. "I love you, Vin."

"I love you, too."

The image of his smiling face seemed to stay there even after he shut the door. I turned away and faced the kitchen, and the rest of my day started to unfold like any other. I fed the boys, changed Vince again, cleaned up the breakfast dishes, made the beds and dressed the boys, let the dogs in and out of the backyard, put a load of laundry in, and folded what was dry. I had my routine down. I was quick and efficient with the chores while the boys played in the family room. *Sesame Street* was on and Elmo's World was ending. That meant it was time to leave the house and go to Sal's new school. It was such a sunny, blue-sky day, I did not want to take the van. Sal had a bicycle with training wheels, and he wanted to ride it all the way to the school. It was about a mile away and since there were no hills, I thought if he got tired I could push him. I put Vincent in the umbrella stroller and we were off. Sal was very good at taking directions. He always stopped at every corner and listened to where I directed him to go. The weather was perfect, a warm, dry day. The sun was shining; it was not too hot. It was just a beautiful September morning.

When we got to the corner of Beach 139th Street and we were about to cross, I remember seeing an Orthodox Jewish woman hysterically yelling at a man: "Look at what they did! It's a nightmare!" She was frantic. We lived in a predominately Irish Catholic/Orthodox Jewish neighborhood, and I thought that something might have happened in the Middle East. I figured something bad was going on somewhere in the world. Our world was so calm and serene, I didn't really give it too much thought. I was busy making sure Sal was safe as we crossed the street.

I was so impressed with Sal. He was not tired, and we were almost there. This was the farthest he had ever ridden on his own. I could not wait to tell Joey how well Sal had ridden. Joey loved to ride his bike and when he could, he would ride it to work. The firehouse was near the Brooklyn Bridge, which was at least ten miles from our house. I knew Joey would be so proud of Sal. I smiled at the thought of telling him about this morning's trip to school.

A few blocks down we made a turn toward the bay and I saw the Manhattan skyline. There was black smoke coming from what appeared to be one of the Towers. What was this? I stopped to really take notice. Was I seeing it correctly? Was one of the Towers on fire?

No, it was not just one; I could see two distinct plumes of smoke coming from both of them. As we neared the entrance of the school, which had a direct view of the Towers, Sal said, "Look, Mommy, a fire."

"Yes, I see it. Daddy is probably there helping people get out." Joey had to be there. The guys from his firehouse were the first to respond to the terrorist bomb at the World Trade Center in 1993. I also had a feeling inside that was telling me that he was there.

As I entered the walkway to the school I saw my friend Kas walking with her daughter Clara, who seemed anxious.

"This is unbelievable."

"The fire?"

"Vinnie, don't you know what's happened?" Kas looked at me like she could not believe my ignorance and explained that a plane had hit one of the Towers. "It's been all over the news. On my way here, I saw another plane hit the second Tower."

I could hardly comprehend what she was telling me. But I had seen the smoke. We lived in Belle Harbor, a part of Rockaway, which is a peninsula—the Atlantic Ocean on one side, Jamaica Bay on the other—with a perfect view of the Manhattan skyline.

When the reality of what Kas had said hit me, I felt sick. I had a pain in my stomach and an overwhelming need to speak to Joey. "I think Joey's there," I gasped.

We were supposed to wait at the back entrance of the school while the teachers took Sal and Clara up the stairs to the classroom. I gave Vincent a toy.

"From what I heard on the news, they think it was done by terrorists," said Kas. "The planes were commercial planes with people on them."

Blood drained from my face.

"Are you sure Joey's there?"

"It's just a feeling."

"You should call him."

I fumbled the phone out of my bag and dialed the number. It was busy, so I called again—same thing.

"Let's go outdoors for better reception," suggested Kas.

Outside I dialed and dialed, but the busy signal continued. My breath was shallow; I had to talk to Joey. Now! I needed to hear his voice. I had to tell him how well Sal rode his bike. He needed to pick up the phone and reassure me that all was well. Busy, busy, busy, busy. In a matter of minutes I must have called him a hundred times. Other wives were probably doing the same. I went back into the school and watched Vincent play and asked Kas everything she knew about the planes and how and when it happened. Then we heard the teacher screaming: "Oh my God, they fell, they fell, take your children and go. They fell!" I felt like I was going to throw up.

As the teacher watched the scene unfolding through the picture window, she kept screaming: "Take your children!" I had to get Sal out of there as fast as I could. I thought of what I had told him about Joey being at the fire, and I was hoping he did not make the connection. Chaos—the teacher running down the stairs with children all around her, parents crowding the stairs trying to grab their children, the teacher screeching: "Take your children! Oh my God!" As soon as I got hold of Sal, I swept him up into my arms, hoping he would feel calm and secure. He held on tight to me as we hurried out of the school basement.

Outside, I saw it: a cloud of smoke where the Towers used to stand. All I could think was Joey was there. I put Sal down and reached for his bike and put Vincent in his stroller. Kas was reading my face. "Can I help? I'll drive," she said not waiting for my reply. "Get in." I felt like I was watching myself—as if I were watching a movie, detached from any reality. I know we threw the bike and the stroller in the back of Kas's minivan, and we buckled the kids into their seats, and then we were off.

Part of me wasn't present. I was disconnected. The only thing I was connected to was my phone, and I continued to try to get through to the firehouse, to Joey, but it was still busy. We decided to go to the local firehouse on Beach 116th Street. Maybe they knew, maybe they could help? Kas pulled up. I jumped out of the car and ran into the firehouse. "I'm Vinnie Agnello. I'm looking for my husband. He works at Ladder 118. Can you help me find out where he is? Is his company at the World Trade Center?" My voice cracked. I couldn't get my breath. I felt as if they looked at me knowing something and did not want to tell me. No one could look me in the eye. They said they had no way of knowing so I left feeling even more scared and panicked. I was sure Joey was there and I was desperately searching for someone to tell me I was wrong.

I remember Kas dropping me at my house. She stayed with me for a little while but her older children were being dismissed from school early so she had to go. I was outside with the boys. I saw that my neighbor Mary's car was in her driveway. I walked to her house. Her husband was also a firefighter. I knew that he also worked in Brooklyn. I wanted to see if she could call him and get some information for me. She was able to get through to her husband. He told her that there was a fire in Brooklyn and that Joey could be there. This should have given me hope, but it didn't. I needed facts. My heart raced. My head felt full of air. I needed someone official to tell me Joey was not at the World Trade Center. The only way I could have hope would be by talking to someone at his firehouse, or by hearing Joey tell me he was not there.

I walked back to my house and gave the kids lunch. I knew that Sal and Vincent could feel my energy, so I tried to distract them with toys. What I really needed was someone to come into my house and take the boys to a calm environment. I needed them taken anywhere not near me, or the news coverage on TV, which I was now glued to, huddled near the screen, ignoring the boys. They had never known me to be like this. I worried about how they were feeling, but there was nothing that I could do to be a calming presence.

I was using the TV for information and was getting angry watching the Towers repeatedly fall. "I've got it already," I screamed. "They fell! How many times do we need to see this?" Adding to my frustration was the fact that we did not have cable and only one network was left broadcasting. All the other networks' antennae had gone down with the Towers. My only source of information and connection to Joey was CBS news. I hung on every word the newscasters spoke, and I prayed they would talk about Joey's firehouse. They had the power to bring me joy or despair. For the first time in my life, the story and the images I was watching involved me. I knew this was a huge news story, but this was my life. I was scouring the TV for pictures of Joey. I knew his character and expected to see him putting others before himself, carrying people to safety. When Joey took his oath, I knew he took it seriously and would never walk away from his responsibilities. I convinced myself that Joey couldn't call me because he was busy.

The phone rang and my heart started racing. Could this be the news that I had been hoping and praying for? Instead it was my mother-in-law. I desperately needed help, someone to be there for the boys and me, and I knew that it would not be coming from her. She told me she had been watching the news and asked me if Joey was home. Knowing how she would react, I spoke to her as calmly as I could. "He's at work." I wanted so much to reassure her and give her the news I knew she wanted to hear, but instead I had to tell her the truth. "He might be at World Trade Center." I could hear the phone drop and then all I could hear was her screaming and crying. My fear at that point had to be put on hold. I had to reassure them. My father-in-law picked up the phone. I told him what I knew and that I was sure Joey would be okay. I did not think that he bought it, but I was trying hard to be positive. I promised that I would call the minute I got any information.

Shortly after I hung up with my father-in-law, my mother called. She has a bipolar condition and had been manic for the past month; I took great care when she was in this state not to upset her. I had to remain calm while speaking with her. I did not want her to pick up on how I was feeling, but I already knew she could feel something was wrong. She always knew when I was distressed. I could be a thousand miles away and not speak with her, and she would know. She said that she was going to come over and help with the boys. I told her not to come, that we were okay. In her present condition having her at my house would be anything but soothing. I took a deep breath. I was able to calm myself with the knowledge that we lived forty-two miles apart. She was a horrible driver so it would be at least two hours until her arrival. Even with that knowledge, I still found that I now had two reasons to panic. I prayed for help: I needed to know that Joey would be okay and that my mother had changed her mind.

Thank God. All the highways to the airports were shut down, and since my house was near JFK, I was safe. She could not drive beyond Suffolk County. This was a brief reprieve. About two hours later, she called again. "VinnieCarla, what an ordeal I went through. By the grace of God I made it home. I have to go lie down now." She never asked if I heard from Joey or how the boys and I were doing. Ironically, I was finally having some luck.

I did feel touched that even in her manic state she had tried to help, but I knew it was better for her, as well as for me, that she was at home resting, and not at my home. Her illness and ordeal temporarily protected her from reality, and I was grateful for that.

Alone with the boys I thought about how lonely my life could be without Joey. He was everything to me. We were a good team and at a point in our lives where we were like one person. We could tell what the other was thinking and have a conversation just by looking at each other. We had counted on each other for everything. He was the first person I called in a crisis, and now I needed him and he was not here. I had no back-up. There was no one else in my life I could really count on. Joey was it. With this realization, a pain gripped my stomach like a vise.

He had to be coming back. The alternative was too overwhelming. I would speak to him soon. He would be home tonight from work. We would have dinner. My life would go on as usual.

When the phone rang again, I grabbed it. It was my friend Joan who had run into Kas. She was calling to see if I needed anything. She offered to come over and help with the boys. She lived five minutes away, so a wave of relief came over me. When Joan arrived she knew exactly what to do. She took the boys outside to play, so that I could be alone. I devoted my time to watching TV for any signs of Joey. She stayed for dinner. The boys ate well, but I had no appetite. After dinner she suggested that we all go outside. It was a warm clear beautiful evening.

I was afraid to leave the house in case the fire department called, so she suggested I leave the phone on the windowsill of the front porch so that I could hear it if it rang. We sat on the porch and watched the boys play, and I waited and waited for the phone to ring. Every minute that went by made its silence louder.

It was around seven p.m. when finally it rang. With my heart racing, I grabbed the receiver. It was Richie, a firefighter who worked with Joey. I knew him well.

"Richie, where is Joey?"

"Vinnie, I am not going to lie to you. It doesn't look good."

"Is he there?"

"We don't know where any of the guys from the Ladder are," he said, confirming everything I had felt since early that morning. I felt like I'd just been sucker-punched in the stomach.

I thanked him for calling and asked him to call if he had any news. I said all of this calmly and then I hung up the phone. I turned to Joan, "He is missing." My legs collapsed; and in that split second, screaming and crying, I fell into her arms. A crowd of neighbors started to gather outside the front of my house, and I heard someone say, "Bring her inside." That's when I realized where I was; pushing back tears, willfully composing myself, I walked into the house. I wanted to hide. I was in so much pain, there was nothing that anyone could do or say that would make me feel better. I wanted to disappear.

Joan took the boys into the family room, and I stayed in the foyer for a few minutes; I needed time to breathe. I walked into the living room and looked at our wedding picture—how happy we were that day. Gazing at Joey's smiling face, I decided I would remain positive: He would come home. Just because he was missing did not mean he was dead. I thought of our life together and all we had to look forward to. I would not give up hope.

Joan agreed to stay with me while I got the boys to sleep. It was around nine p.m. when I realized that she had been there all afternoon. "Do you need to go home?" I asked. She said she could stay. Relief. I had spent plenty of nights alone in my home while Joey worked night shifts as a firefighter, and I had always felt safe, but not now. I was stuck in a nightmare. I needed to have someone there so that I could talk and be distracted. I felt jittery. My heart skittered. My breathing raced. Adrenaline controlled me. I couldn't eat, drink, relax, let alone sleep. Joan knew I was in shock. She had known me for three years so she knew my baseline, and I was far from it.

The first time I met Joan, Sal was two weeks old. I took him to the chiropractic office where she worked because he had colic and would not stop crying. I had been so stressed as a new mom because he never slept and he cried all the time. When I had called the pediatrician, he told me not to worry about it and that Sal should stop crying at around three months. Three months seems like forever when it comes to a crying baby. I was desperate and had heard that the chiropractor in our neighborhood had adjusted infants and that he might be able to help Sal. I was practically in tears when I took him there and Joan had comforted me. Both Sal and I were adjusted by the chiropractor, and Sal finally stopped crying. Afterwards Joan held Sal in her arms, and he actually fell asleep. There was an instant connection between them. She was the mother of three grown children and she knew a lot about home remedies, natural healing, and breast-feeding. Joan walked into my nightmare that day, September 11, 2001, and gave me the helping hand I so desperately needed. We watched the news and then talked all night. I was wired, like I'd had ten cups of coffee, so I did most of the talking, telling her all about Joey and how we'd met.

It was December 16, 1989, and it was cold outside. I was tired. I had worked all day and the idea of going to bed was so appealing. I put on my pajamas and was ready for bed when my phone rang. It was my friend Victoria calling to see if I wanted to go out dancing. That was the last thing I wanted to do, but she told me to take a nap and she'd call back later. Typically, we would leave after ten o'clock at night, and it was only around dinner time. I agreed to nap and see how I felt. Several hours later, Victoria called, waking me, and even though I did not feel at all like going out, something inside pushed me. At around ten p.m., we were on our way to our usual nightclub, Metro 700, but at the last minute I whipped the car into the parking lot of a nightclub that was having its Grand Opening— not because I was looking for a new club, but because I was afraid I would run into a previous boyfriend, Mr. Wrong, at Metro 700. Mr. Wrong and I always ran into each other at Metro, and I really wanted to get on with my life. I also just wanted to go out have fun with my friend. I was not on a mission to meet a guy.

We walked in to blasting dance music, just like any other club. We checked out the dance floor—not that big. Still, it seemed like a nice place. I was just glad that I would not be running into *him*, but as I looked out onto the dance floor there he was. It was Mr. Wrong dancing with a girl! Just my luck. I wanted to leave but we did not have enough money to go to another club. Victoria wanted to stay, so after a brief argument in the ladies room, Victoria suggested I walk up to him and let him eat his heart out. She felt I was having a great night as far as looks go. I did look good that night. I had on a new black dress that fit me well in all the right places, and even I had to admit that I was having an exceptionally good hair night, but it was not my style to act like a bitch. I had no intention of going up to him. I wanted him out of my life. I agreed to stay for her, but I would do the mature thing: I would hide.

I was sure he had not seen me, so I spent the better part of my night staying out of his sight. If he was heading in one direction, then I dashed in another, which is no easy task in heels. There were times that we almost came face-to-face, but I avoided disaster, teetering into the crowd or dodging behind a dividing wall. At one point I almost fell over. I just could not be discovered. In an effort to keep ahead of him, I spent most of the night looping around the place in big circles.

I never ran into Mr. Wrong, but I did keep running into another man. He was tall and handsome and had the most beautiful eyes. It seemed that wherever Mr. Wrong was, the handsome stranger was in the opposite direction. I must have looked ridiculous to him, trying to look casual as I hid and dodged. I was sure that he thought that I was stalking him or that I had a mental illness. When Mr. Wrong finally left the nightclub, I found myself standing across from the handsome stranger; I was camped by the bar, hiding. I took a deep, relieved breath and as I exhaled, our eyes met. My pulse jumped, my face flushed. This was not just attraction; something else was going on. For a moment it was like we were suspended in time, and it was in that moment that I felt like I had known him from somewhere. But certainly I had never met him. There was no way I would forget such a face. It was such an odd feeling of familiarity, but it made no sense. When we both turned our eyes away, the feeling of knowing him stayed with me, but I told myself that it was not possible. You don't just run into a man you have clearly never seen before and know him already.

Since I could make no logical sense out of it, I turned to my twenty-two years of life experience and what I knew to be true of handsome men: He had to be a conceited jerk, most likely had a girlfriend at home, and was clearly out with friends looking to cheat. I had him all figured out, and I was sure I would not run into him anymore, since I was no longer hiding from Mr. Wrong.

Victoria and I danced for a while but we were getting tired and bored so we headed toward the door. Just as we started out, the tall, handsome man put his arm in front of me and said, "You are not going to walk past me again, are you?" I laughed and he smiled at me. He had a great smile and there was a kindness about him that I could feel. I felt a sense of comfort in his presence. I felt safe. We started to talk, and I started to feel the sense of having known him again. I could also tell that he was genuinely a good guy. When he said that he was from Sheepshead Bay, Brooklyn, I almost laughed, because he was proving every theory of mine wrong. Almost every time my friends and I had gone out to a nightclub on Long Island, one of us met a loud, obnoxious guy who said he was from Sheepshead Bay. Nothing about this guy made sense in the world of men I had known. He was so easy to talk to, and we clicked right away.

While we were talking, one of my favorite songs came on and as if he knew, he asked me to dance. We danced together for a while until a bad song came on. He offered to buy me a drink—as a rule I did not allow guys to buy me drinks. I always drove, and I always wanted to be in control, especially in a nightclub. I let him get me some water. I asked him if he could tell me his name again. The music had been so loud when we had started talking, and I did get distracted when he said he was from Sheepshead Bay. "Joey," he said grinning.

Before I left he asked me for my phone number. Usually I would have a pen, but since it was not my intention to meet a man that night, I was not prepared. All I had was black eyeliner, and I wrote my number as clearly as I could on a bar napkin. It was already smudging when I gave it to him.

This was the story I told Joan that panicked night in 2001, as we waited for word about Joey. I told her that on the car ride home from the dance club, I knew there was something special about Joey.

I remembered telling my girlfriend back then about the feeling I had when I looked into his eyes. She was into psychics and astrology and believed in the unexplainable, so she understood what I was saying. As I drove, I thought about the bar napkin, and I prayed that the eyeliner hadn't smudged.

⁂

Joey called me three days later, the perfect amount of time to wait. The very next day would have meant he was desperate, and the day after that could imply the same, but the third day meant he was balanced and cool. He knew the unspoken rules of dating, but he did feel comfortable telling me that he got a pen right away from the bartender to rewrite my number before it became illegible. I loved that he shared that with me.

Christmas was a few days away, and our days were busy, so we spoke on the phone several times before we got together. With our work schedule conflicts, we settled on a first-date lunch. I had been working for Calvin Klein in the men's fragrance department at the A&S department store in Manhattan. It was cold out, and I only had an hour for lunch, so with little choice, we headed for the food court in the mall. I had butterflies in my stomach and was not sure I could eat the hamburger I had ordered. I had forgotten how handsome he was. My nervousness fell away as I looked into his big brown, kind eyes and we began to talk. Being with him was easy. Our conversation flowed, and he had a great sense of humor. I was really enjoying myself so I was caught off guard, when he asked me, "So how many brothers do you have?"

Panic! He was initiating a "tell me about your family" conversation. How would I tell him the truth? My mind flashed to a previous boyfriend—about six months earlier. It was the evening I had just come home from Stony Brook University Hospital. I had been there all day waiting for my mother to be checked into the psychiatric unit. She was not there voluntarily. The day had started early around six o'clock in the morning. When I got home, it was nine at night. That night, the boyfriend broke up with me because he did not want to go out with a girl who had a mother like mine.

Sitting there at lunch looking into Joey's eyes I thought of what to say to him. Should I tell him that I had spent most of my childhood wishing to be part of the television families like the *Brady Bunch* and *Little House on the Prairie*? Did he need to know that I lived most of my early years in fear of my father's explosive temper, or how my home was like a war zone with my parents on opposing sides?

Of course I could not tell him all of this. I would just tell him why I was not living at home. I could explain that since my father's death almost five years earlier, it had become necessary for me, on occasion, to leave my home. But should I tell him it was because my mother would get so confused she would attack me physically? Maybe, but I would leave out the details of how she came at me with knives. Could I tell him how my friend Dean helped me move by throwing my belongings into a Hefty bag while Mom was out of the house so I could go somewhere safe to live? I don't think so. Each time I left I would go to different friends' homes, or I would rent a room, or live in a room at a friend's house. That was my current situation.

Was this really the time to tell him these truths? I felt such a connection to him; surely I would be gambling if I told him all of this. Would he get up and run? I was not sure. I was hoping he might be the answer to the prayer I had made a couple of months before. Could he be the man from the wish list I had written? If he was, he would be able to handle the truth. One thing I knew for sure: I did not want to go any further, or invest any more time with someone if I had to hide my life. But I struggled. Would he be able to see me? Would he be blinded by my circumstances? Something in my soul told me that I could trust him. Like an ocean wave crashing against the rocks, my fears flooded the space between us. All of this caused by a simple question about siblings!

I took a deep breath, looked into his eyes, and gave him the shortest and most honest explanation: "You seem like a really nice guy, so I can't lie to you. I live with my friend Tommy, his mother, and younger brother. I have my own room in their house. The first time you called, my friend Tommy answered the phone. I'm sorry he was rude, but he is very protective. The second time you called, it was Tommy's brother who answered the phone. The other guy who answered when you called last night was my friend Dean. Tommy,

Dean, and I have all been friends since we were in junior high school. I have never dated them. We are all just friends. The reason I live at Tommy's house is because my mother suffers from a mental illness. She gets abusive when she gets sick. She is a really good person when she is well, and I love her, but she gets sick often. Her illness seems to have been caused by our financial circumstances. She worries about losing our home. When my father was dying of heart disease, he lost his mind near the end and cancelled his life insurance policy to be spiteful. Our house was paid for but she was left with no money. I do have one brother and he lives with her. We are very different and not close. I'm sorry that I lied and said Tommy and Dean were my brothers, but it's kind of a hard situation to explain over the phone."

It had all spilled out, so quickly—like a nuclear accident! I was waiting for him to get up and run. Instead he surprised me. "I can tell you are a really nice person. I like you. I have no reason to judge you. I would like to get to know you better."

I fell in love with him at that moment, and I knew someday we would be married. Joey was unique. He had the ability to look beyond the dysfunction surrounding me. He could see just me.

Joan reached out and took my hand. The long night of September 11, 2001 was almost over.

September 12, 2001

I WAS SO GRATEFUL TO JOAN; SHE STAYED UP WITH ME THE entire night. If she was tired, she hid it well. Adrenaline in full force, I could not cope alone. The rising sun brought hope. I felt safer. In my mind, it felt like my nightmare would be over now. I believed in this new day.

Joan stayed and helped me give the boys breakfast. She had noticed that I was not eating. When she offered me food I refused it, so she gave me some water. It had been a whole day since I had eaten, and I hadn't even noticed. I could no longer feel thirst or hunger. Joan followed me around constantly telling me to drink; I did so out of a sense of obligation to her, rather than a feeling of need.

It was around seven o'clock in the morning. I remembered where I was supposed to be, if things had been normal. I was a registered nurse, and I was supposed to be at work. I worked in a big hospital in Manhattan as a per-diem maternity nurse. "I should be at work and Joey should be here with the boys," I told Joan. I wanted so much to blink and to have things back the way they were, but nothing was the way it was before.

I told Joan that I would be okay if she wanted to go home. She looked at me and asked if anyone was coming to help. When I looked into her eyes, I could tell what she really wanted to ask:

"Where is your family?" I told her that I was not expecting anyone and left it at that.

Alone with the boys, I could feel their rising sense of fear. I had no reassurance to give them. They wanted my care and love. They had a desperate need to be nurtured. I was incapable of giving them emotional support. I knew they were looking to me for stability, but there was nothing stable about how I felt, so I provided them with what I could: I gave them food and made sure they were clean and dressed. I was going through the motions like a robot and I know they felt it. I wanted to give them so much more, but I truly had nothing to give.

My energy went into preserving our family, and I did that by watching the television for signs of their father and by praying. Acting like a triage nurse in a hospital emergency room, I prioritized the greatest need, and the greatest need was to get Joey back. The only way I knew how to do that was through prayer. It was all I could do. Praying to have Joey home became my mission. It was hard to do that with the boys around. They were whiny and restless, picking up on my energy. I put them in the family room with their toys, but they wanted my attention. I wished someone would come and take care of them so I could fully concentrate on the quality of my prayers.

There was a knock on my door. Thank God, it was my neighbor, Dawn, offering to take the boys for a while. Sal and her son were the same age and often played together. I knew that the boys felt comfortable with her. What a difference twenty-four hours had made. It was only yesterday that I was sad at having to part with Sal for a couple of hours at nursery school and now I readily handed both sons over. I was no longer the mother they had known the day before.

With the boys gone, I had no distractions, and I went back to praying and watching for signs of Joey on TV. He had to be okay.

With no news from the firehouse, I watched the news even more intensely today. They were showing new footage with images of survivors being rescued from the rubble. When would Joey appear? I scanned crowds for his mustache, his uniform, anything that could identify him among all the other people. I was afraid to blink, to look away, to have my attention anywhere else because I did not want to miss seeing him. After an hour or two of watching the same footage over and over, I started to drift off to sleep. When I woke, I thought I had slept for hours, but it had been only ten minutes.

Now it was noon, and I thought how long it had been since I had said goodbye to Joey. About thirty hours, but it felt like years. I thought of every detail prior to that moment. I could still see Joey playing with the dogs before leaving for work, and talking with Sal and Vincent. I could hear him asking me what was for dinner and what he, Sal, and Vincent were scheduled to do the following day while I was at work. I thought of the night before and how making love with him was always so good. I thought about his medal and how it would sway back and forth across his chest, occasionally hitting me, something we would both laugh at. He wore his medal of St. Florian, the patron saint of firefighters, at work. It was a gift my mother gave him when he graduated from the fire academy. I could still feel how it felt to be in his arms, and I could still smell his scent.

I thought of how even after twelve years together there was nowhere else I wanted to be than in Joey's arms. I knew every detail of his body—he was thin and muscular, he had sculpted arms and a defined chest, he had long lean legs I called "bat legs," because they felt like wooden baseball bats—and I loved every inch of his body.

In my mind I went back and remembered every single detail of September tenth. I could see the whole day: I'd had a dentist appointment, and the plan was that Joey would meet me there and take the boys to the playground. He was coming from a study group he had with some firefighters. I arrived at the dentist office early, and Sal had a conversation with one of the dental assistants. She told me how nice and polite Sal was. I remembered the pride I felt and how eager I felt to share it with Joey, knowing the pleasure he, too, would feel. All the love, time, and attention that Joey and I had given the boys showed in their actions.

Joey picked up the boys, and when I was finished at the dentist, I called him. Within ten minutes I could see all their smiling faces in the van as they pulled up to the curb. We talked as we drove home. Joey told me about the park and how the boys played, and I told him about the compliment and how sweet and polite Sal had been. As we drove over the bridge into Rockaway, I remember how the angle of the sun reflected off the water. It was so lovely and bright, it seemed to mirror our lives.

When we got home that day we played with the boys and then ate dinner. The boys loved eating just as much as their dad. Nothing pleased me more than to watch all three eating with such enthusiasm. As the boys ate, I told Joey about something that had occurred that day. "I felt my father's presence around me, in the car, as I was driving the boys to the dentist. This song came on that he liked, and I could feel him sitting next to me. It's kind of weird, don't you think?"

"What's weird?"

"That he would be around me for no special reason."

"I'm not sure I'm following you, Vin."

"Well, the only other times I've felt him so strong, like today, were our wedding day and when the boys were born. The other time I felt him was that night I was in the car accident."

"I don't remember."

"How can you forget that? It was all I could talk about at the hospital when you picked me up. Well, I will never forget it. I was at that red light, and I saw headlights in my rear-view mirror. Then I heard the van smashing into the back of my car. It was like time was suspended for a moment, and that's when I felt him. He was in the front passenger seat of my car, and I heard him say in my mind, "YOU'RE GOING TO BE ALL RIGHT." Then in an instant I could feel the car going out of control, and as I felt the impact, he was gone. It was miracle that I was fine."

"I know it was. I remember how totaled the car was. It's amazing you didn't get killed."

"I felt like my father protected me that night. Why would he be around today? It's not a special occasion."

"Maybe he just wanted to see you and the boys."

"You think I'm nuts, Joey?"

"No, I don't. I know you are!"

"Very funny."

"I believe you. I do."

"So why do you think he is around?"

"Maybe he is here early for Sal's birthday."

"Forget it, Joey. I know you don't really believe in all this."

"Maybe he just wanted to see what an amazing mother you are."

"So foreplay is starting already?"

"Why not?"

I kissed his mouth and whispered, "You know where to find me later."

"Let's just hope your dad is not around later."

"You're disgusting." I tossed a dishtowel at him.

I got up and started to clear the table and Joey got up to load the dishwasher. He had two helpers behind him. With Sal and Vincent's "help," it took him twice as long, but he was always so good with them. I loved watching how he treated them, always with patience and kindness. He was a natural when it came to being a father.

Joey planned to study after dinner. He was already on the list to be promoted to lieutenant, but he wanted to keep current with information and take the next test. The boys were interrupting him too much, so I decided to take them for a bike ride in Fort Tilden, a local park. Joey could study in peace and quiet. He helped load the bikes into the van and buckle Sal and Vincent into their car seats.

We arrived at the park. With Sal on his bike, I put Vincent in the baby seat on my bike and off we went. We rode our bikes around for a while, and it started to drizzle, but we were still having a fun time so we kept on riding. When the rain got heavier, we went back to the van and I put the boys in their seats. It was not easy to lift my bike and angle it to fit inside the van. After I managed to position the bike in place, I was able to load Sal's bike and we were on our way. Two blocks away from our house, I stopped at the traffic light in front of our church. Looking ahead, I saw a familiar car. It was Joey, in our Honda; we smiled at each other and rolled down our windows.

"What are you doing?" I already knew he was coming to help me.

"When I heard the rain, I thought you might need help with the bikes."

I could still see his smiling face so clearly. Joey came to my rescue, as he always did.

But it was today: September 12, 2001. And the comfort I got from thinking of Joey turned into overwhelming sadness when I realized I did not know where he was. And then it hit me: Joey was the one who needed to be rescued, if in fact he was still alive. An alarm went off in my head and I quickly said "Sorry" to God and the universe for thinking for a moment that Joey might be dead. I had temporarily lost faith, and I did not want God to get angry. I still had such a powerful connection to Joey. I felt he needed to know I was not giving up hope. Somehow this would help him with whatever ordeal he was going through. In my mind, he was buried alive with all the guys from his ladder company; but he was holding onto the energy I was sending to him. I would be his lifeline. I prayed and tried to send him my good energy for the rest of the day. That got me through day two.

Around two o'clock in the afternoon, the boys came home. I tried to spend time with them but I was distracted, and they could feel it. I wasn't functioning as the mother they knew. All of my motherly instincts were replaced with fear and panic. The patience, love, and security that surrounded the boys evaporated. With the falling of the Towers, the very foundation of their lives and mine had collapsed. The best that I could do when they were in my care was to put a video on TV for them. My energy was manic, and they were picking up on it. They got whiny and agitated easily. I am sure they felt their mother was missing along with their father, even though neither was capable of verbalizing it. I needed help, but there was only one person I could have counted on, and that was Joey, and he couldn't be found.

I was starting to experience a feeling familiar to me, but one which was part of my past, never my present—the feeling of being left alone. I knew it all too well. It came with chaos, and it was never intentional. It was just chance, and in the past it had come through family circumstances, like mental illness and heart failure.

The Fog

FOR THE NEXT FEW DAYS MY LIFE PASSED IN A FOG, I WAS still not eating or sleeping. My body had no need for these basic functions. The one thing that was getting me through the days was the firm belief that Joey would come home and we would be a complete family again. I would not allow myself to doubt this.

From the moment I had met Joey, my life had changed for the better. He was a true friend. He would do anything for me. It was early in our relationship when I'd had the car accident with my father's presence so palpable. I had been at Joey's house and I was on my way home that night. I always called him when I got home so he would know I was okay. After the drunk driver crashed into my car, I was taken away by ambulance, and when I got to the hospital a nurse called Joey for me. I was badly bruised and had a terrible whiplash, but I was lucky to be alive. The man who towed my car thought I had been killed; the car had been so badly mangled. Joey waited with me at the hospital until I was released and he drove me home. Since my car had been totaled, I had no car. I did not have money to get another one. Joey and I had been dating six months when this happened. I loved him, and I knew he loved me, but I was shocked when he told me to take his car. He said he didn't need it. He was working in Manhattan at the time, and he commuted by subway. He still needed his car, of course, but he knew how important it was for me to get from the suburbs to work. Joey never made me feel like I owed him anything. He had my back. When we were newlyweds and I returned to college to become a nurse, he told me I did not have to work while going to school. Although we were broke, he told me to do well in school and not to worry about working. I was taking a lot of classes, and he did not want me to be stressed.

From the night when we first met, Joey had always been there for me. Where was he now? But I would not allow doubt. I would not for one second think that he could be gone.

Joan and my neighbors continued to come over in shifts to help me. Some took the boys for the day and others stayed with me overnight. After a few days, the fire department put together a phone line that family members could call and get updated hospital lists or a list of the deceased. I called every hour on the hour and thanked God, deeply relieved when Joey was not on the deceased list but disappointed that he was not on the hospital list. The only outcome I would permit in my head was that he would be found and in a hospital. To prepare for the call that he was on the hospital list, I went to his armoire and took out his favorite T-shirt—a gray one with navy blue trim—his favorite jeans, his socks, underwear, and sneakers. I put it all in a duffle bag and placed it on my dresser so that it would be ready when I had to leave the house for the hospital. The image that continued to come to me was of Joey hurt in hospital with his left leg broken. I just felt that something on the left side of his body was not right. Every time I called the fire department, I prayed hard that they would tell me Joey had been found, was fine, and would be coming home.

He had to be. He promised me that he would never leave.

Somewhere in the fog of the first days after September 11, 2001, I grew weary of watching the news footage. I was restless. I needed to walk, but I could not leave the house. It was one o'clock in the morning. The boys were sleeping in their beds. The dogs were asleep by the front door. It was a mild September night, so I opened our front door and sat down on our steps. It had been five years since I had sat in that same spot, at almost that same time.

I had awoken then thinking about the miscarriage. I'd felt a sense of hopelessness and sadness that I could not shake. I was no stranger to pain and suffering, of course, but there had always been a resiliency I could tap into, even in the worst times. This time the old resiliency wasn't there. I felt empty. It had been twenty-four hours since I'd lost the pregnancy. I couldn't sleep and did not want to wake Joey, so I'd walked quietly from the bedroom and out the front door. The waves were crashing on the beach, and I could see as well as hear them from the front door. It was so loud, as if I were standing right on the beach. There wasn't rain in the air, but the wind was blowing a salty mist into my face. I felt comfort in the sound of the waves crashing. They mirrored how I was feeling. I sat alone on the steps and cried. Just then, I heard our front door open.

"What are you doing out here by yourself?" Joey slipped in beside me.

"I didn't want to wake you. I was thinking about the baby. I feel so empty." I wiped the tears from my eyes.

Joey put his arm around me. "Why didn't you wake me? You shouldn't be alone."

"I feel bad about what happened."

"I do too. It was my baby, too. You should've woken me. You are not in this alone." He pulled me closer.

"I didn't want to upset you."

"Vinnie, I love you. I need to know how you're feeling. You don't have to feel this way alone. We are in this together."

"I know, Joey, but there is nothing you can do to make me feel better." I leaned into his strength.

"I know, Vin, but I can sit next to you and hold you. I am always going to be here for you. We can get through anything together."

I remember telling him that night how much I loved him and hugging him for his loss. We sat there for twenty minutes, silent, listening to waves crash. Joey's arms were around me. I felt sad, but comforted, too. I knew then that if I fell, Joey would always be there to catch me.

Prayer

AS EARLY AS I CAN REMEMBER I HAVE FELT A CONNECTION TO something greater than myself. As a child I always felt that I had some sort of guiding presence with me, and there were times I could sometimes feel and know things before they happened, thanks to this presence. Raised as a Catholic, I felt that the guiding presence I had always felt had to be God. The God I was connected to was not like the God I sometimes heard about in church, who was severe and punishing, but more a force of love in line with the stories of the life of Jesus and his compassion. I never had to be in church to feel this presence. It was with me all the time, but I did find when there was trouble at home I liked to go to church because it was quiet and peaceful.

In 1985 when I was a senior in high school and my father was dying, both of my parents' mental health had deteriorated. They had always argued with one another, but that year, with both of them suffering from different types of mental illness, our house seemed to overflow with rage and anger. For peace and guidance I went to church every morning for the six o'clock Mass. I knew that my parents were incapable of giving advice or paying attention to my needs, so I was taking care of them; in church and through prayer, I felt as if God was looking after me.

In the summer of 1989 when I was living at a friend's house, his mother received a statue of the Virgin Mary that she was told to pray to for a week before she was to pass it along. She asked me if I would pray to the statue with her. My mother had been sick for a while, so I was feeling bad and thought it might help. It was said to my friend's mother that whoever prayed to this statue had good things happen to them and she felt that she and I could both use some help. At first it seemed strange, but there was something peaceful about the statue. We prayed in front of it every night for the week that it was in the house, and although I still felt a little foolish, I started to feel a sense of comfort. While the statue was in the house, nothing dramatic happened. But about a week later, I was at a bookstore and was drawn to an aisle in the back, to the very bottom shelf, and to a book that changed my life. It was called *The Power of Positive Thinking* by Norman Vincent Peale. It was a small paperback, but there was something huge about the book that seemed to be calling to me. The book was about having faith and a positive outlook. It showed how to gain access to a greater power, even for the most mundane daily tasks. I had always prayed for guidance but never for anything specific. This book taught me how to pray for whatever I needed and also said that I could have a lifetime of happiness. Up until that moment I was just going along taking what life dealt, and although I was in college and on the path to making a life for myself, I never thought that I had any real control over creating happiness for myself. Peale was a Protestant minister, and his ideas were very different from what I had learned as a Catholic. He wrote about positive visualization and only believing in the best outcome beforehand. It made sense to me, and I started to apply some of the concepts to my daily life, and my life changed for the better. I went from feeling powerless and scared to feeling confident and optimistic.

I started to use prayer along with hard work in my daily life to attain goals, and I found that it always worked. Before that I would never have thought of using prayer to get what I wanted. After it started working, I started to pray for everything. I even prayed for a wonderful man. The book spoke of the power of writing things down, so I made a list of qualities that I wanted in a man and I believed that when the time was right, God would send him into my life. Shortly after that I met Joey.

As time went on, I continued to use the principles of positive thinking. Everything that was good in my life was there through hard work and prayer and through a belief that I could have it. Whether it was the nursing position in the hospital of my choice, the house of our dreams by the beach, or the ability to work per diem so I could have a flexible hours, it was done through prayer and positive thinking. Sometimes things were not answered the way I wanted, but things would always work out better than I expected.

Every day that Joey was missing I prayed to God. I prayed to the Virgin Mary as well. I prayed to her purposely to prove to Joey that God did exist. I was hoping that she would appear to him while he was waiting to be rescued. Joey did not pray as a rule and did not really embrace my belief. He was raised a Catholic as well, but only went to church when obligated. When he did go, he was like a bored child, often looking around at the stained glass windows and the statues, and if he prayed at all it was for the Mass to be over so that he could get the hell out of there. I was amused by it and never tried to change him. I would just share my point of view, and whenever I found anything inspiring, I shared it with him.

In July, I had read a book called *Stolen Lives: Twenty Years in a Desert Jail* by Malika Oufkir, which I thought showed a good example of a higher power existing. The book was a true story about a family in Morocco who was imprisoned for a crime that was committed by their father. I told Joey about a part of the book that I found amazing. The family was Muslim, but when they were in trouble, the Virgin Mary had come to their aid. The reason I told Joey was that I thought he would be impressed that they were not Christian and had no reason to prove that the Virgin Mary existed. She gave them many signs during their time in prison, and she had even appeared before one of the women. I was hoping not only that Mary could help Joey, but that he would then know there was a higher power there to help him.

The whole time Joey was missing, I had been praying to Mary, and she seemed to be sending me signs that she was there. One afternoon a few days after Joey was missing, my neighbor Mike came over. "I don't know if you are religious, but my brother is. He gave me this a while ago, but I think you can use it more than I can. It's a prayer card with the Virgin Mary where she appeared in Medjugorje."

"I've been praying to her," I told him.

"Then you've got to have this," he answered and gave me the card.

I kept a statue of the Blessed Mother on our windowsill above our kitchen sink. After I had spent the better part of my day in front of the television looking for Joey, I felt overcome with fear and started to cry. When I went over to the kitchen sink to splash my face with cold water, the statue of Mary fell into my hands. It had never moved before.

Another night, about a week after Joey was missing, I was up late in our family room, unable to sleep. I was exhausted, but my body was still running on adrenaline. I started to say the Hail Mary over and over again, and I eventually fell asleep. When I woke a couple of hours later, I noticed a scribble mark that had been on our wall made by one of the boys months before appeared to be in the silhouette of Mary. It was the same exact mark but it seemed to have changed overnight.

Another neighbor knocked on my door one morning and gave me holy water that her daughter had brought from Lourdes where Mary was said to have appeared. I had awakened that morning in a panic thinking of Joey and had prayed to Mary asking her to help calm me. Later, looking through a family photo album at pictures of Joey, I started to feel scared. I turned the page, and there was a picture of Joey, his nephew Sal, and me at his first communion. We were all standing in front of a statue of Mary, and it looked like she had her hand on Joey's shoulder.

No matter what anyone else might think, I knew that during one of the darkest periods of my life, my prayers were being heard. What the outcome would be, I was still unsure, but I knew that I was not alone and neither was Joey. One evening I heard a knock on the front door. One of my neighbors had brought over meatballs and sauce. She also had cooked a plate of pasta, and she handed me a Ziploc® bag with grated cheese in it. I took her gift and thanked her. As I put everything in the refrigerator, I looked at that bag of cheese and thought of Joey.

I could see us all at the table again. I had just cooked dinner and set the table. Sal perched in his chair. He was nine months old. I gave him some spaghetti. Joey was waiting and I had just sat down, too. Everything was on the table, except the cheese.

"Vin, can you get up and get the pecorino?"

"I just sat down. You know you are perfectly capable of getting it yourself." I smiled at him as I said it because I did find it funny that he was so spoiled.

"Please, Vin. You're closer to the refrigerator."

"You know, Joey, I should have married a Jewish guy." He knew why I said that. I would often tell him stories about the husbands of my patients (the majority of whom were Jewish), running around at their wives' beck and call.

"You would be so bored. You love the stallion. You could never be satisfied with any other man."

"Oh, so now you're a stallion. How long have you thought of yourself this way? You are a spoiled baby."

"You know you love the stallion, Vin. You love that I'm untamable. You crave the stallion."

"Oh yeah, Joey, are you an Italian Stallion?"

"I'm your stallion, and you can never be mad at me, because I'm adorable."

He was joking of course. He did not think of himself as an Italian Stallion. In fact being Italian was not something he talked about, but he was right about me. He knew me so well. I could never love another man. "The Stallion" was the perfect man for me, faults and all. It became our private joke and whenever he did anything that pissed me off, he would say, "You love the Stallion." And it always made me smile. No matter how angry I was at him, whenever he said it, I would laugh and forget to be mad. Oh how I loved him and his silly humor.

All that brought back by a small plastic bag of cheese. I could never let go of Joey. I prayed harder.

After several days with no news, I realized I had to pray even harder. That was the only way that I could save him. If God could just see that I had a strong faith then he would have to let Joey live. Eating and sleeping were still difficult, as prayer became my main focus. One afternoon, I dozed off for a few minutes and when I woke, I remembered a hymnal that I had seen in church as a child: "He who sings prays twice." I was starting to feel so desperate that I thought God needed to hear me twice as loud; I had to turn my praying up a notch. I had to sing.

I thought of the song "Bring Him Home," from *Les Misérables*. I had seen the show on Broadway with Joey and loved the words. While the boys were asleep, I found the CD and played it. The song is a prayer that the lead character sings to God asking that his daughter's love will live after he is wounded in combat. "God on high / Hear my prayer / In my need / You have always been there . . . Bring him home / Bring him home / Bring him home." I could barely sing. I was choking with tears. The score and song captured what I felt in my heart. A part of me felt so stupid and desperate. My voice was hoarse and weak. I could barely talk, let alone sing, and I was afraid someone could hear me through the window. I shut the windows and continued to play the song over and over and over again. It felt like it was my anthem, my last hope of reaching God and saving Joey. The nights were the worst time for me. It was when I was left alone that my thoughts turned negative. Because I wasn't sleeping, the nights also brought loneliness—nights were the only time Joey and I'd had alone. So I spent my nights praying and singing ever more intensely.

I was relieved when the sun came up; it brought me a sense of hope and optimism. If in a moment of weakness I doubted Joey was alive, I would apologize to God. I would then picture Joey in the hospital with a broken leg—always his left leg—and we were all around his bed, happy that he would make a full recovery. I felt that what was happening was a test of my faith and that I could not waver in my hope for his return. I had to remain positive; I had to hold on to this belief because I was Joey's lifeline. I owed it to him to be strong. If he was in a hole and waiting to be rescued, he needed my energy to hold on to.

Sal and Vincent

SALVATORE, OUR FIRST-BORN, WAS JUST FIVE DAYS FROM HIS third birthday the morning that Joey last left for work. I knew that part of being a good mother to our little boy now meant telling him the truth. As the days went on, it had been getting harder and harder to keep telling him, "Daddy is still at work." I was aware that Sal had witnessed the phone call the night of the eleventh when I fell into Joan's arms and he also knew that I had not been able to get in touch with Joey. Sal also knew that if his father was going to stay at work, he would always say hello to Sal on the phone. I had asked Joan if she had any advice about what to tell Sal, and she said she would talk to her friend who was a child psychologist.

The psychologist's advice was to be truthful with Sal, but to keep it as simple as possible. I explained to him that his father was missing and that his dad had helped people that day, but the fire department did not know where he was. I also let him know that I thought his dad would be fine and that he could pray with me for his dad to come home. I tried my best to explain about God and praying and Sal understood it the best he could. He did pray with me and asked God to bring his daddy home. The way he prayed broke my heart: "Please let my daddy come home today, God," he would say in his little voice. He understood that his dad was not able to contact us.

Sal also knew that it was not normal for his dad to be away this long. He did not cry about it because I told him that Joey would be coming home. I did say that I did not know when his daddy would come home, but that I was praying it would be soon.

Sal did not want to go back to nursery school and I could not blame him. He remembered the teacher screaming and he had watched the collapse from the window, so I decided not to take him back there ever again.

As Sal's birthday had approached, I was flooded with thoughts from three years earlier. I had missed my appointment with the doctor two weeks before my due date. Later, at work, I ran into her. I had one of her patients as my patient and when she saw me, she said I was looking very big. I was thirty-nine weeks pregnant, and she said that she wanted me to come to her office on my lunch break. Her office was in the hospital. She wanted me to have a sonogram. It showed that the baby was too big. There was no time to wait. I was scheduled to be induced the next day.

Joey and I arrived at the hospital around noon. They gave me a drug to help induce the labor. It was taking a long time, and as we waited, Joey began getting hungry. There were a bunch of restaurants and delis that delivered to the hospital. I suggested that he have food from a Spanish place. They served chicken, rice, and beans. I knew he would like it. He called in our order from our room, and we waited for my labor to start and for his food to be delivered. I was starting to have contractions but the pain wasn't bad, and I was pretty comfortable.

When Joey's food arrived, my doctor came in and broke my water to help move things along. After she left, I started to have a lot of pain. Joey and I never took a class on having a baby, because I worked in maternity. I felt I knew what to do. I tried to breathe through it, but the pain was getting bad. "Joey, it hurts!" He didn't hear me, though, because he was enjoying his food. "Joey, I'm in pain! Get the doctor. I need an epidural."

"Okay. I'll go tell your nurse."

When he got back, he told me the anesthesiologist would come as soon as she could. He went back to eating as I counted between contractions.

"Vin, this is the best. You have to try it."

"Joey, I can't take this pain? Where is the doctor?"

"Soon. The chicken is so moist and the beans and the rice are so good. You really have to try this."

"Thanks Joey—not a good time. I'm in pain!"

"Okay, but this is really good, and I think you should have just a taste."

"For God's sake, Joey! I'm in agony over here! I'm happy you like the food and want to share, but I've never felt pain like this. Could you get the doctor? Now!"

At that moment the anesthesiologist came in and put in an epidural for the pain. When Joey saw that I was feeling better, he started to talk about the food again. "Oh my God, Vin. I can't believe you're not going to try this."

"You enjoy it for the both of us. I love you, Joey."

The induction didn't work. The baby never went into the birth canal. There was no alternative, and I had to have a C-section.

Sitting there in our house waiting for Joey to come home, I could still hear him as excited about the baby as he had been about the food. "Vin, it's a boy. He's beautiful! You have to see him, Vin. Oh my God, Vin, you have to see him! He has big eyes, and he has a lot hair, and his feet are big. You have to see him. He's beautiful."

I could still see Joey smiling, and I laughed thinking about him and the Spanish food and about the day Vincent was born, too.

Vincent was due when Sal was nineteen months. I did not want to be away from Sal too long. I was hoping for a vaginal birth. I went into labor on Sunday, April 16, 2000. Sal was exactly nineteen months old. Joey drove me to the hospital at ten p.m. My contractions were ten minutes apart. When I arrived at the delivery room, my colleagues came in to visit. I was in good hands, and since I was not ready to have the baby, the doctor said Joey could go back home to Sal and we would call him when I was closer to delivery. Joey went home, and all night and most of the morning my friends popped in and stayed with me. Around six thirty in the morning, the doctor told me to call Joey. I would be having the baby soon.

Joey got there just as I was starting to push the baby out. Some of my colleagues were there with him—all cheering me on. When the baby failed to come and an intense pain started to rise from my lower back, the labor nurse and the doctor realized that the baby was posterior (head up, instead of down). This meant that the delivery would not only be painful, it would be long. I was told how intense the pain would be and how long it would take to push him out. A Cesarean would be a good option. I was stubborn and said I could handle it. It was very painful, and at times I would push so hard that my blood pressure would get very low. I was getting weak. The doctor, who was also a friend, said he could easily get the baby out via C-section, but I continued to refuse. He said it was my decision but if it got too difficult for me he could perform a C-section. I pushed when I could, and my friends came in and out of the room. My legs had been in the stirrups for hours and I was in so much pain that I had forgotten about Joey's fears about the delivery room. When I was pregnant with Sal, he'd informed me he would not be looking down when the baby came. He did not want to see me all stretched out. He was afraid it would be a sexual turn off. Around the fifth hour of pushing, when I was taking a break, Joey and I were the only ones in the room. He came over and settled my gown between my legs.

"Joey, no one cares. We see this every day. I'm fine."

"Yeah, but I don't want to see it anymore." We laughed so hard we cried.

"You tried as hard as you could," he said when he'd pulled himself together, "but I'm worried about you. I can't watch your blood pressure drop again. Please, have the C-section."

He couldn't take it anymore. I didn't realize how much he was suffering watching me suffer. I was in physical pain, but he was hurting emotionally. I could not have that. I suddenly got a rush of energy like I could move a mountain. I told him to call the doctor and the nurse. "I am going to push this baby out right now!" I pushed as hard as I could and felt the most awful pain. I was exhausted and all I could see was Joey. His eyes were full of tears. "It's a boy."

Our little boy Sal turned three years old on September 16, 2001. I never told him. It would have broken his heart to have a birthday without his daddy by his side, and I didn't have the strength to let Sal feel that absence on his special day. It broke my heart that the picture I had held in my mind of Joey in a hospital bed with Sal and Vincent nestled at his sides and everyone eating birthday cake had not come true.

I knew Joey wanted to be home for Sal's birthday. He wouldn't miss it for anything. I figured we would celebrate it when he got home.

Family Support

WITH THE EVENTS OF THE PAST WEEK, MY MOTHER SNAPPED out of her mania. She loved Joey like a son, and I believe her deep concern for him, and for me, somehow triggered a change in her brain chemistry. She genuinely tried to be supportive of me. She offered more than once to come and help, but because of her lack of good driving skills, coming to my house was not an option. I thought it was best that she stay home. I was the one who took care of her. She was not at all capable of taking control of things, and we both knew it. I was also concerned about my grandmother. She had Alzheimer's disease and was in a nursing home, and my mother visited her every day to help take care of her, even when she was manic. I felt my grandmother needed my mom. Besides, Mom was not able to function away from her home, without getting nervous, so having her around would have just added more stress. I was simply relieved she was back from her mania and I could talk to her again. I was hoping as I always did that she would stay well, not check out again, but her mental state was anything but stable. Still, I spoke to her every day and I felt comforted that for now she was there for me and praying for Joey.

The Rest of Our Family

MOST OF MY ENERGY WENT INTO CARING FOR THE BOYS AND praying for Joey. Whatever I had left went to tending to our beloved dogs. Chelsea and Durante definitely felt Joey's absence. They were suffering right along with me.

Of course, they were not just dogs to us. They were members of our family, and Joey and I could not have cared for them or loved them more if they had been human. We got Chelsea the first year we were married, when Joey was in the fire academy and I was finishing college. Joey had wanted a boxer ever since he was a boy and said he would feel better working nights knowing Chelsea was there with me. A breeder in New Jersey had a litter of puppies and we went to see them. One in particular, the leader of all the others, chose Joey. She gave him the leaf that she was carrying in her mouth and later she fell asleep with her head on Joey's sneaker. She was ours. At home we put her to bed on the floor next to us. Our lives quickly revolved around Chelsea. Everything we had done previously now included her. Nothing would be planned without thinking how Chelsea would fit into it.

When she turned two, we had to breed her as part of the agreement when we bought her. It was hard for us because she was our baby and we didn't want her to go through a pregnancy. The night she had the puppies, she went into labor quickly. Joey and I were like two mothers fussing over her. It was like we were there to deliver our first grandchildren. When the first one arrived, we were by her side. Then three pups quickly followed. After a short time, I had a feeling there was something wrong; Chelsea was restless and could not settle. I looked into her eyes and I could see her struggling although she appeared fine. I told Joey that I felt that she still had more puppies inside. He assured me that she was fine. I told him I could feel that something was terribly wrong. He was on his way back to bed when I went into our room and started to get dressed. "I'm taking her to the emergency vet in Bay Ridge. I'm sure that something is wrong." It was one o'clock in the morning. He knew I was going with or without him. He looked at me through his exhausted eyes and said, "Okay, Vin, I'll drive." We quickly put all the pups in a basket, threw a blanket over them, leashed Chelsea, and rushed her and her pups to the emergency vet, who X-rayed her. There were four more puppies and Chelsea needed a C-section to deliver them.

There was only one doctor and one assistant on duty, so when the vet found out that I was a nurse and Joey was a first responder, she asked if we could be there to assist them. When Chelsea was being prepped for the surgery, I was in the room. Joey left. I followed him. "Come on, Joey. They need our help." His sad eyes looked into me, and I could see his pain. I knew what he was going to say. "I can't go in there. I can't see her like that. I can't be there. I'll stay with the puppies." He sat down next to the basket and watched them. I had never seen him like that before; he loved Chelsea and clearly didn't want to see her cut open. I realized at that moment how sensitive he was; here was my big, strong, brave, firefighter husband, not afraid to walk into a burning building but absolutely unable to take a step toward seeing his beloved Chelsea in any harm.

She had eight puppies that night: four females and four males. One puppy in the litter was not only a character, but he displayed a deep attachment to Chelsea. We called him Jimmy Durante because his snout looked big.

Everywhere we went, we took the dogs, even on vacation. We only went to hotels that allowed dogs and we only went where we could drive. People thought we were crazy the way we treated our dogs. They said we would change when we had kids, but when we had the boys, our feelings toward the dogs did not change at all. We were just a bigger family.

After the boys were born, Joey was the prime caregiver of the dogs, so now in Joey's absence Chelsea and Durante were confused and suffering. Not only was their daddy not there, but I had nothing to give them; the best I could do was to let them out into our small backyard.

The Unknown

EVEN AFTER A WEEK OF HIM GOING MISSING, MY FAITH THAT Joey would return was strong. However, my body was weaker. My throat became tight, like it was being strangled and on fire. I developed laryngitis the day Joey went missing, and my voice was always hoarse. My body was still not allowing itself to rest either, and I still had no appetite. I ate little. I hardly drank water. I was losing weight. In the seven days since Joey had been gone, I had slept a total of ten hours. I felt lightheaded like I was in a fog.

One night I dozed off between Sal and Vincent while putting them to sleep on my bed. I dreamed I was in the exact same position on the bed. In the dream I woke up and standing at the foot of the bed was Joey. He had no shirt on. He smiled and walked toward me. "Don't come any closer! If I can see you then you must be dead."

He smiled at me and came closer to our bed.

"Please stay back! What are you doing here? If you are here, then that means you are gone."

He stopped. "I am not gone, and I am not going to leave you."

Then he lay down next to me on the bed in a fetal position. I relaxed. I felt I could breathe. I felt so comforted by him, and once again I could sleep knowing he was with me. When I woke up, Sal was lying next to me in exactly the same position as Joey had been.

The impact this dream had on me was huge. I believed absolutely that Joey was alive and that his spirit had come to me to let me know he was alive and would be coming home.

I now believed that his body was trapped and soon he would be found. So convinced was I that I couldn't wait to tell Sal the good news.

The Firehouse

During the previous week, I had not left the house unless it was to pray at my church around the corner. The guys from Joey's firehouse, Engine 205 and Ladder 118, had asked if I would come over and bring the boys for a visit.

Joey had been a firefighter at this firehouse for eight years, and he was part of a second family. Over the years we had all shared a lot of fun together, from summer picnics to Christmas parties, dances, and weddings. I was not surprised when they called and invited us. Seven other firefighters from Joey's house were also missing. The guys were concerned about all of the families. They had been searching for seven straight days for their missing brothers, and it was important for them to reach out to their families. Since I was still not sleeping and was in no condition to be driving, my neighbor Joanne offered to drive the boys and me to Joey's firehouse in Brooklyn Heights. It felt odd to be out of the house and on the Belt Parkway. We weren't going over the speed limit, but still it felt too fast, too overwhelming for my senses. My eyes could hardly adjust to the colors all around me, from the cars racing past on the opposite side of the road to the light reflecting off the water, and yet even though I did feel dizzy, it felt good to be out of the house. I had almost forgotten there was a world. As we drove past the spot where we would normally see the Twin Towers, it seemed so surreal. The road was familiar, but foreign without its marker. Instead of two impressive towers, all I could see was a smoldering hazy cloud of smoke. Gone was the landmark that I had known all my life. Whenever the Towers were on my left, I knew the exit to Joey's firehouse was coming up. Their absence left a gap in the skyline, my inner map, and my heart.

When we arrived at the firehouse, the garage doors were open and surrounding them were hundreds of flowers, candles, cards, notes, and stuffed animals spread out on the sidewalk. I had known I wouldn't be walking into the firehouse of old, the one I had known and loved, but I wasn't ready for this. I had only been there when Joey was working; the last time was when Joey was in his summer work duty outfit, my favorite. I loved the way his skinny legs looked in those navy shorts. I could still see the image in my head—the navy shorts, his black socks, and big shoes coming toward me, a huge smile on his face. It was a sight I loved, the perfect combination of sexy firefighter with a touch of old man because of those black socks. Joey was happy when he was at the firehouse, and even though it was a dangerous job, he loved it. The guys in the firehouse, like a real family, were often arguing and making up. The firehouse was full of male energy, and there was always a lighthearted, playful vibe in the air. Perhaps it was because at any moment they could be put in a dangerous situation. They liked teasing each other and pulling pranks. For me the firehouse always meant seeing Joey, or being together as a family at the Christmas parties that were always held there. It was a place I liked to be.

But as I walked past the flowers that lined the garage doors, I felt a wave of sadness. This was a different place. As I glanced around at the faces I had known, I was struck by the change. They looked hollow and beaten up. Their eyes told their story, and their pain was obvious. Some found it hard to look directly at me. They seemed to be struggling to keep their composure. Others spoke openly. Some spoke only with their eyes. All were full of compassion. I appreciated it and loved them for all they were doing, but I hated feeling like the object of pity. I wanted them to know that Joey would be home soon and back at work, and that it was okay if they had given up, but I hadn't.

I knew that a total of three hundred forty-three members of the FDNY were missing or reported dead, and that eight of the missing were men from Joey's firehouse. At the firehouse, I listened to their descriptions of how the events unfolded. The five firefighters who worked on Engine 205 from Joey's firehouse were sent to the World Trade Center within moments of the first plane hitting the North Tower, which was at 8:46 a.m. They stopped to take a firefighter from another firehouse to an ambulance parked a few blocks away. The firefighter had been struck by the body of person who had fallen or jumped from one of the towers. Despite their efforts the firefighter died, but as a result, the men of Engine 205 lived because they were diverted from the Towers. Still, they were almost buried alive from the falling debris. The fire truck, Ladder 118, that Joey worked on was held back until 9:02 a.m. and then dispatched to the World Trade Center. The only facts the guys knew was that Ladder 118 did arrive at the World Trade Center and that the truck had been found parked on Vesey Street with its windows broken and its cab filled with twisted steel.

They told me of their enormous effort to find their missing friends and colleagues. One firefighter, a friend of Joey's, had been climbing into dangerous holes looking for them. Other guys dug through smoldering rubble. Everyone had risked their lives trying to find survivors, as well as their fallen brothers.

Since September eleventh, they had been working twenty-four hours on duty and twenty-four hours off duty. Some of them just stayed at the firehouse; they were too worn out to go home just to turn around and come back again. They, as well as their families, were suffering. They were not sleeping. They were exhausted, and they had no time to grieve because their services were so desperately needed.

On top of that, they were now dealing with the families of the eight missing men. The firehouse had become a focal point for most of the relatives. Family members of any of the missing men would turn up at the firehouse on any given day.

While I was at the firehouse, I was asked to sign paperwork, giving the department permission to obtain dental records and DNA samples, which would be used to identify Joey's remains, if needed. For a moment, I felt the impact of what that meant. My stomach twisted, my chest tightened. It was a painful glimpse of what I could feel if Joey was actually found dead. I could not think of Joey in terms of his remains, and I quickly put the thought out of my mind. I signed the papers knowing Joey would be coming home soon, and the papers would be unnecessary. I felt comforted with this thought.

Part of me wanted to pretend Joey was gone, just so they wouldn't think I was crazy, but I couldn't do it. I had to remain loyal. I was his lifeline, and he needed me not to give up. I knew people were looking at me as if I had lost my mind. I was getting used to it, but I knew I was right and they were wrong. I hoped he would return soon, but it was becoming increasingly difficult for me to convince people that he was fine.

The longer I stayed at the firehouse the lonelier I felt. I hated that Joey was not there with me. It did not feel right being there without him. It was his firehouse. I wanted him to be helping with the rescue effort. I kept expecting him to walk in and take his place with his friends. I wanted my life to be the way it had been before. I could feel a deep sadness in my heart, and I wanted to cry, but I couldn't do it. I did not want to upset the guys any more than they already were. The last thing they needed was to see me crying. My throat was tight, my stomach in knots, and my head was hurting. I swallowed hard to fight back the tears and not one fell, but I had to get out of there.

I wanted to run, but instead I walked slowly and calmly with Vincent in my arms and Sal's hand in mine. As I started to make my exit, I noticed Joey's name along with the other missing men from the Ladder still written on the chalkboard with the riding order for that day, as if suspended in time.

As I walked out of the firehouse, I turned back to re-envision the last memory I had of Joey: smiling—navy shorts, black socks, big shoes. I tried to keep this picture in my mind, but it was overwhelmed by row after row of flowers, stuffed animals, cards, and candles.

Getting Out of the House

FOR THE FIRST TIME IN OVER A WEEK I FELT COMFORTABLE TO leave the house. Joey's colleagues had given me a cell phone, donated by Verizon, when I was at the firehouse. Now they could reach me when they got news of Joey. I felt like I had some freedom, so I decided to take the boys to Fort Tilden, my favorite park, near our home. Since it was my first time driving in over a week, I took things slowly. I packed some of the boys' favorite toys and Sal's bike. I also took the bag with Joey's clothes, just in case I got the call that he was at the hospital. I took a fifty-dollar bill given to me by Joey's cousin. She lived a couple of blocks away and stayed with me one night during the first few days he was missing. I had no money on me the night she was over and, since then, I had not gone out or spent a dime. My neighbors were sending food, had purchased diapers and groceries for us, and I never left the house. I had no idea how I was going to pay our bills since neither Joey or I were working, but I didn't think about it. I was just trying to get Joey back; it was the only thing I could focus on.

I was happy to get the boys outside. It was such a perfect fall day, and I did not want to be on our block. I couldn't take the look of pity I felt some people gave me. I hated feeling paranoid, but as soon as we were out of the house, I felt as if I were being watched.

It was as if I was going out for the first time after a prolonged illness. My legs were shaky and I moved slowly. The park was only five minutes away, so even though I wasn't sleeping and was kind of in a daze, the drive would not be dangerous. It would be quiet at the park. No one was ever around during the week, and I wanted privacy.

As I entered the park, I could see a charity organization collecting money. The closer I got, I could see they were collecting money for rescue dogs. I learned the money was going to the aid dogs that were searching for missing people and remains in the rubble at Ground Zero, the new name for the World Trade Center. Special boots were needed for their paws and other specialized equipment was necessary. Without hesitation, I reached into my back pocket and gave them the fifty-dollar bill. Only two thoughts went through my mind: it is in giving that we receive, and, what you put out comes back to you.

The weather was beautiful and for the first time in days I was able to be present for the boys. There were even moments that I forgot Joey was missing. The boys seemed to be having a good time. I chased them, and they laughed, and then we all sat down for a picnic under the trees in the cool shade.

As we sat, my mind wandered. My eyes caught the sight of the volunteers, and I felt the panic come back. I had to get back to the house. The boys would be ready for a nap soon, and I could get back to praying. I packed up the car and we headed home.

When I pushed open the front door, money and checks flew all over the foyer. I had a mail slot, and it seemed that in my absence my neighbors took the opportunity to stick cards, checks, and cash through it. There was well over five hundred dollars in cash and checks. I cried as I picked them up off the floor. I did not recognize some of the people who had left checks, and I was touched that they knew who I was and that they cared. I was also struck at how fast the money that I had given out had come back. The money I had given away came back to me tenfold. I was reassured that I could now buy diapers and the food we needed. Joey would be happy to know that people cared about us while he was missing. I knew he would be home soon and we both would be able to work again, but for now I could pay our bills.

Point Pleasant

I NEEDED TO GIVE THE BOYS SOME SENSE OF NORMALITY. JOEY and I had planned a day trip to Point Pleasant, New Jersey, for the twenty-second of September. We had been there about a month earlier and had had a great time. It was a nice family place on the Jersey Shore with a boardwalk, rides, and an aquarium. Since we'd had so much fun, we had planned our return trip while we were eating dinner.

We loved that Sal and Vincent were so independent and fearless. They were only one and two and a half, but they had no trepidation. They went on all the rides and laughed. Other kids their ages cried and wanted to get off the rides, but not our two. They were having the time of their lives and so were we. Joey and I would catch each other's glance and smile with pride as we shared in our sons' excitement. I could not remember the number of smiles we gave each other that day, but I remembered well the happiness we shared.

As the twenty-second approached, I decided to take the boys back. I promised myself that I would do the things we had planned. I knew that Joey would want us to go, and I pictured myself telling him all about it while we visited him in the hospital. I could see the image of Joey smiling and laughing when I told him about our boys on the rides and my bravery of going alone without directions. I called the firehouse the night before to tell them where I was going and to make sure that they had my cell number in case I needed to get back quickly.

On the morning of the twenty-second the weather was perfect, the air was dry. It was sunny and warm. I took this as a good sign. I had asked some neighbors if they wanted to come, but they were nervous about driving over bridges. They were afraid of more terrorist attacks.

As I got ready, I remembered our first trip and how organized Joey had been. He had made peanut butter and jelly sandwiches the night before and packed fruit and water for all of us. He put the cooler out the night before and had it all ready to go in the morning. Joey loved family outings and made sure we were super organized.

I was relying on my memory to get us there. I knew we took the Garden State Parkway, and I knew the name of the exit, but for the rest I would have to rely on my instincts. With no traffic, the drive went smoothly. The journey turned out to be easy. I remembered the route exactly. I even parked on the same street in the same spot where Joey had parked a month earlier. I felt proud of myself for making it there and I was hopeful we would have a good day, but as I unpacked the car, I realized I had forgotten the sandwiches and I was instantly mad at myself. Joey would never have forgotten the food.

It would be fine, I told myself. I would buy the kids some lunch at one of the food stands. My confidence returned as I put the kids in the double jogger, but immediately, as I made my way to the boardwalk, I felt alone. Memories of our last visit washed over me: how happy we had been, how much enjoyment we had from being there together. As panic spread inside me, I longed to retreat to the car. Press on, I told myself. It will be fine. Joey wants the kids to have fun. But as I walked the boardwalk, the emptiness grew so huge I felt as if I were going to be swallowed up. Everywhere I looked I could see scenes from our earlier visit. Families surrounded us. Where was Joey's friendly face and his smile? Where was he?

His absence in my life started to feel real, and I was getting scared. They will find him. They will find him. He will live. He will be back. But the reality that he was not there hit hard. I prayed in my head: They will find him, they will find him, they will find him . . . but when? Oh God, I don't think I can take this anymore. I am okay, I am okay. I can do this, I can, I can.

We got to the amusement park, and I bought tickets. Sal and Vincent seemed happy. I put them on their first ride—a little boat that went 'round and 'round. I waved and smiled at them and then turned right, a natural reflex, to see Joey's reaction. But he wasn't there. The boys were waving and ringing the bell on their boat, smiling back. I kept looking for Joey to smile back, too. Where was he?

They will find him, they will find him . . . I waved and smiled to the boys. He will live, he has to, I know he will, thank you, God, for letting him live . . .

☙

I was in a daze—not quite there—as I walked around putting the boys on rides. The sun was strong and I began to feel shaky. Thankfully the boys were distracted and having too much fun to pick up on how I was feeling. They saw their favorite fire truck ride. It was not crowded and they wanted to go.

"It looks like you have future firefighters on your hands," the woman running the ride said as we approached. I laughed and told her their dad was a firefighter. I continued without emotion: "He is missing right now."

The woman's face fell. "Not the Towers?" I nodded and wished that I had not said anything because I did not want to upset her. I also was aware that her sadness and worry were triggering my fear. "Don't worry," I told her. "My husband is strong and healthy and will be home soon." She looked at me with pity, like I was crazy. No one understood! They didn't know what I knew—that Joey was coming home.

I thanked the woman for the ride, but wanted to get as far away from her as possible. We headed to the other rides until we were down to our last ticket. I went back to the booth and bought more. As I started to walk away, a man who worked there approached me. "Are you the woman whose husband is the missing firefighter?" he asked.

"Yes."

He took my new ticket book, gave it to the woman in the booth, and returned my money. Then he gave us wristbands and said the owner of the amusement park wanted us to be his guests. The owner wanted to meet us, he said, if that was okay. I said I was more than happy to meet him.

Since this man was kind of old, I figured the owner would be a really old gentleman. I knew that the amusement park was family-owned and operated, but was surprised to discover the owner was in his thirties, like me. He introduced himself saying he was a volunteer firefighter and had two boys a little younger than Sal and Vincent. He introduced me to his wife and boys. They were a lovely family and reminded me of us. They asked if I needed anything.

"No, we're fine. Thank you." And then I told them how happy Joey would be to hear of their kindness. I promised I would return with him so he could meet and thank them in person. They smiled as I said this, but there was a look in their eyes that had become all too familiar.

I didn't want any more talk. I wanted to get on with my day and keep the mood happy, but the reality of being without Joey surfaced when I needed to use the restroom. The door to the entrance was too small to fit the double stroller and I couldn't take the boys in with me. Such a small thing, but the impact was huge. Just weeks before, Joey had watched the boys while I went to that same bathroom, not a care in the world. Suddenly, his absence felt mammoth. I wanted to flee to the car and hurry home. But a girl who worked at the park was walking past, and she agreed to watch the boys. Grateful but wary of a stranger watching the boys, even briefly, I went quickly.

When we returned to the rides, Sal and Vincent wanted to go on the helicopter. The last time we had been there, Sal could not hold the button down, so instead of the helicopter going in the air, it stayed on the ground and just went 'round and 'round. Joey and I yelled to him: "Press the button!" But he was too little to get it and we laughed. "Someday he will figure it out," said Joey.

When I put Sal and Vincent on the ride, I expected to see a repeat of the last time. Instead, Sal pressed the right button and up they went. Hooray! I was so excited. I laughed and turned to see Joey's beaming smile. Instead, empty space. All of my excitement and happiness faded; he should be here! Why isn't he here? Where is he? Damn it! He missed it. They better find him soon.

Soon it was just too much—the forgotten sandwiches, the bathroom, the helicopter. I wanted to cry. My mind could hardly comprehend all the sadness that was welling up inside of me. There was a pain in my heart, and I wondered how long I could bear being without him. He should be here. This is all that he wanted in life: a happy home, a wife, two beautiful children. His family was growing, and he and I had all that we had dreamed of, and now he wasn't here. My brave face was weakening, and now I felt as if I were being tortured. Still, I thought that I could go on. I reached inside deep down and told myself I would be okay, I could take the boys on another ride. This one was for adults, too, so we all could go together. As we started up in the air, a strange sensation came over me. My sense of sight became altered. I could see the boys' smiling faces, colors swirling around me, and an empty seat next to me. All three images were clear to me at the same time like three different movies all playing before me. The empty seat then overshadowed the other images; it was the seat that Joey should be sitting in. It grew and grew until I wanted to scream. Oh my God! Where is he! This cannot be my future, not an empty seat, not a life that Joey is not a part of. I prayed: He has to live, dear God, he has to live, he is too good, he is a great father, he loves these boys, this cannot be.

I needed him, and the boys needed him. I needed to share this experience with him, not be here without him. This can't be real. This can't be my reality. Tears poured down my face, and I tasted salt in my mouth as the ride went spinning 'round and 'round. I barely knew where I was anymore, and I could not control the tears.

I had to get off the ride. I had to get out of the park.

Finally, it was over. I put the boys in their stroller and pushed quickly toward the exit. I was hoping my sunglasses would hide the tears that wouldn't stop. My cheeks were wet and I could hardly breathe. I wished I were invisible.

On the way out, I ran into the owner's wife who could see my distress. The look in her eyes haunted me; it was one of deep compassion for what she knew was missing.

As fast as I could, I got away from the boardwalk and the people. I was sobbing, out of control. I just wanted to get home. Vincent was too young to see that I had been crying. I kept my sunglasses on, and he was happily eating a cracker, but Sal could see that I was upset. I told him I was sad and missed his daddy and I was sorry that we were leaving, but I knew his daddy would be home soon.

"That's okay, Mommy." He gave me a kiss, and I told him that he made me feel better. I put the boys into their car seats, folded up the stroller, put it in the back of the van and started the drive home. I just wanted to fall into Joey's arms and bury my face in his chest. Where was my best friend? I missed him so much. I began to pray: Please, God, don't punish me for feeling sad, I still believe you will bring him home, I was just having a weak moment, I believe he will be found, thank you, God.

As I drove, the boys fell asleep. I was glad, because I was sobbing. I was so scared about what our lives would be without Joey. I had not allowed myself to think about this. I hated it. I hated the sadness. I must pray even harder for my miracle. Time was going on, and I had about nine days until the three week mark that I had given myself.

When we got home, I wanted to put my head down and sleep. I played a video for the boys and tried to relax on the couch. I needed to quiet my thoughts. When the phone rang, I did not pick it up. That's when I heard Joey's voice: "You have reached the Agnello residence. Please leave a message, and we will call you back." I got up and pressed the answering machine button to hear the greeting again. Hearing his voice after ten long days was like balm. I played it over and over and over. It was his beautiful voice—the one that said, "I love you, Vin, so do you want to marry me, it's a boy, we have a son, I will always be here."

The Power of Positive Thinking, Or Insanity?

AT WEEK TWO I STARTED TO LIMIT MY EXPOSURE TO PEOPLE. I only allowed myself to see or speak to people who believed that there was hope for Joey's return. When Joan was over, she screened my calls. One afternoon a friend Joey went to the fire academy with came to visit, unannounced. I knew him pretty well because he had lived in our neighborhood in Brooklyn when we lived there. He now lived a few blocks away from us in Rockaway, and he was also in Joey's lieutenants' exam study group, so I saw him regularly.

"So how are you holding up?" he asked.

"I'm okay. I'm not sleeping, but I know he'll be home soon."

Joey's friend started to reminisce: "I can just see him that day, yelling to people to guide them to safety . . ."

I realized he thought Joey was dead. He'd come to comfort me.

"Joey will be coming back soon. "

He stared at me. "I'm worried about you, Vinnie. I'm afraid you aren't going to be able to accept it if he isn't found alive."

I felt sorry for him for being so negative, and I told him that I had not lost my mind. "I know how serious it is, but I have to keep hoping. If one more week goes by and Joey isn't found, I'll have to accept that he is gone, and I'll have to start to deal with what that means. Not knowing is hell, but when there is no way to know if he is dead or alive, I have to go with the best outcome. The love Joey and I have is too special to give up on so quickly." My throat ached, but I'd had my say.

I told him I remembered reading a story about a man who had survived after being buried alive in an earthquake for three weeks and that it was possible that Joey could still be alive, and for a brief moment I think he could see my sanity.

The Ghost

SINCE THE TRIP TO POINT PLEASANT AND SINCE JOEY'S FRIEND'S visit, I had started to question my thinking. I was exhausted by not knowing Joey's whereabouts. I was still not sleeping and even though I was exhausted I was up late one night. Vincent had had a late nap, so he was still awake, full of energy, and playing with his toys in the family room. I sat thinking about Joey.

A ball that Vincent was playing with rolled into part of the kitchen that bordered the dining room. He walked out of my view into the kitchen on his way to the dining room. "Hi, Daddy. I am playing with my ball. It rolled away."

I couldn't believe what I was hearing. I jumped up and found Vincent. "Who are you talking to?"

"To Daddy."

"Vincent, where is Daddy?"

"He is over there." He was pointing to the dining room, which was pitch black.

"Where is he, Vincent?"

"Right there, Mommy." I walked toward where he pointed, and I couldn't see Joey at all, but it didn't feel normal either. It felt like something was there with us. It was a feeling I'd had before, and it gave me the chills. I did not want to believe it was Joey, but I knew that Vincent was sincere and definitely saw and talked to something.

I left the room. It can't be. I'm just tired. My mind is playing with me; I did *not* feel Joey. Vincent's just a baby with a pretend friend. I put it out of my mind. I wasn't ready to face what I knew it meant if he had come to visit.

The Basement

ON THE MORNING OF OCTOBER 1, 2001, I WOKE UP AFTER sleeping for four hours, the most I had slept in three weeks, and I thought about the significance of the day. This was the day I had been avoiding since the minute I knew Joey was missing. I said I would give it three weeks, and the day I had prayed would never come had arrived. This was the day. I had to face up to the reality of what my life without Joey would mean to me and our two boys. Imagining one day with him dead was overwhelming, let alone a lifetime. It was with this thought weighing me down that I climbed out of bed.

A deep sadness started to fill me, but instead of allowing myself to feel it, I pushed it away. I started to do lots of tasks. I became busy, *very* busy. I felt hyper as if I were going to run a marathon. Jittery. I could not focus on my emotions. I did not want to, so I made sure I did not have time to feel anything. I gave the boys breakfast, then the dogs, and then the cats. I cleaned up the kitchen, did some laundry, and took care of the rest of the house, racing from task to task. I made the beds, dressed the boys, and then I took a shower and got dressed. When I finished one chore, I hurried to another. I did not want to feel what I was feeling. Keep busy. It will go away.

But the reality was that this was the day I was going to have to face the fact that the man I loved and had built a life with was dead. Reality had hit, and I hated it.

It was around eleven thirty a.m. when Joan came over to give me a hand with the boys. As they played in the living room, Joan and I talked in the kitchen. I had finally stopped dashing around and doing tasks. I stood very still in the center of the kitchen.

"Vinnie? How are you doing?"

Joan had seen how quickly I had been working, how fast I was running from room to room. She was well aware of the time that had gone by and knew that I had reached the deadline for holding on. By the way she looked at me, I knew she knew what I was avoiding. During the past three weeks she and I had seen each other or spoken every day. There was an understanding between us. I didn't have to say anything, but I said it anyway. "Joey has to be gone."

Joan had known this, but she knew how important it was that I be the one to say it. As I said the words, my body, as if it were separate from my head, felt the enormity. All the energy I had put into praying and staying positive had been futile, and it had left me exhausted. I was defeated. A great ache and a sense of falling replaced the hope and possibility that had lived in my heart for the past three weeks. Joan hugged me and before either of us could cry, I asked if she would take the boys out for a little while, so I could be alone. It was a sunny day and she was happy to take them down to the beach so they could play in the sand.

After she left I needed a place where I could shut out the world. My body, my mind, my heart throbbed with pain. I needed to be far away from everyone. I needed a cave, but all I had was my basement. As I walked down the stairs, the clenching in my heart filled my throat, my eyes poured, my mind raced—he could not be alive now, even in some hole; it was over, hope was gone, my best friend, dead.

Tears.

Through the blur, I found the washer and the dryer; my chest tightened; a voice in my heart was coming out my mouth: screaming. What was that noise coming out of me? It was like a movie, the past three weeks. I could see myself on my bed, trying to sleep, pleading and begging with God, the same prayer over and over: Please, God, let him live, let Sal and Vincent know their daddy, please let him be okay, please, God, don't take him from us, he's is a great dad and a wonderful husband, he's my best friend, please, God, please, God, please . . .

I heard the screams, louder. "Goddamn it! How could you take him? Why him? Why us? We were so happy! How could you let this happen to such a good man? How?"

There was screaming and crying and then this loud moan. It seemed to rise from the pit of my soul. I couldn't stop it. I couldn't breathe. It was pouring out. All the feelings, all the emotions, from that morning, September eleventh, everything I had bottled gushing out. Pain. All the suffering and anxiety, the waiting, the not knowing once corked, now burst like a bloody gash.

What had happened in the past three weeks? I tried so hard not to give up hope, the repeated phone calls to the fire department, the waiting, praying, sleepless nights, not knowing, news footage, buildings falling and falling and falling, white smoke everywhere. It was all over now, but my tears were not. I was crying and moaning—on and on—no attempt to control it—I am not sure I could have. No one could see or hear me; alone, I was free to feel my pain.

I have no idea how long this went on. All I know is that each scream, sob, and wail released some of the pain that was torturing my body.

Then all at once it stopped. I grabbed some paper towels and blew my nose. I felt exhausted, like I had just relieved tons of pressure from the depths of my soul. I felt released. I should go upstairs. I splashed water on my face. Yes, I would go upstairs, face the world. But I was frozen. I remember just looking around at all of the stuff in our basement. All around me, the evidence of our happy life: the shelves with his fire department manuals and the magazines Joey used as references. Our treadmill, our Christmas stuff, our old furniture covered with pictures and books. Then I spied it, the shopping bag full of bandages. They had been hanging there since Sal's birth. Three years. Joey had had to change the dressing on my incision from the C-section. Because I did not stay in bed and rest like I was supposed to, my incision had opened, and Joey had lovingly taken on the task of changing the bandages—we had so many of them, we did not want to waste the extras so we put them in a shopping bag, and the bag hung from the ceiling. Like a piñata.

I strode to the bag. In my mind I could see Joey carefully lifting and replacing the bandage, his smiling face. I could feel again his kindness—it filled me like light—and I could see our happiness and all that was lost. Our life—and how beautiful it was. A rage welled up in me. The pain, a live beast, more and more anger, some fire inside, ready to explode. I punched at the bag. Hard. More. Punching. Grunting. Yelling.

"Why?"

"No!"

Punching. With all my strength. Crying so hard I cannot see. One more swing, lunge. But I miscalculate. I miss the bag and hit the ground. Cement. Lying with my face on the ground, I curl into a ball, cheek on the hard, cold floor. A puddle of mud forms from my tears. A strange thing happens. I see myself from above. I see myself crying on the cold dirty floor. I could die. A part of me has. I watch the woman on the floor. I cannot move. She just lies there. I think about getting up. She does not have the energy to move. Every breath. Pierces. Pain of reality. Pain of a life without Joey. I want to stay here and leave the world behind. I look down at my image. It is such a strange phenomenon. It lasts a few minutes.

∽

A calm feeling came over me. There was silence within my heart. In that silence I heard a little voice. It was faint at first, but then it grew louder and louder: "Get up, get up, get up!' I found the energy. I sat up and looked around at the mess I had made. Bandages were all over the place, I sat there looking at all of it. It was as if I had been away. Now, when I looked around at the mess, I knew I had to clean it up. I got up and started to clean. As I cleaned, I started to pray: "God, since Joey is dead, I hope he died quickly. I hope he was never in pain."

I carried the tattered bandages to the garbage, talking to God, but talking to Joey, too. I told both of them I did not understand why this had happened. "I'm going to need help raising two boys alone. I'll be the best mother I can, but I'll still need your help."

I remembered a conversation Joey and I had had about a week before September eleventh. A young New York City firefighter had died while on duty and Joey, who never missed a funeral for a firefighter, had gone to Staten Island to pay his respects. When he got home, he told me his feet might be hurting from his shoes, but he was so glad he was not the one in the coffin. I said that he must never leave us. "I need you with me. The boys need their father."

I reminded him about the time he'd overheard me giving Sal a piece of toilet paper to wipe himself after he'd peed. Joey had been shocked. He'd rushed into the bathroom. "Sal, you just need to shake yourself." He'd been so glad he was there to show Sal what to do. He'd laughed when I'd reminded him of this. I told him I was grateful he was in our lives.

"Don't worry. I will always be here."

"Good," I said, "because I don't want to live in a world if you're not in it."

Conversations about Joey dying seemed to be a recurring theme, whether it was because he was a firefighter and the job had dangers, or because there was something deeper inside us that had a knowing, I couldn't tell.

I remembered, too, the day he had come home from the funerals for two of three firefighters, all fathers, who had died in a fire in Astoria, Queens, on Father's Day. He'd told me that if he ever died he wanted me to move on with my life and remarry someday. I told him that I could not do that, and then he had gotten real serious. "Vinnie, you have to promise me that if something ever happens to me you will go on with your life, you will remarry. You and the boys should have a good man in your lives."

"Stop it, Joey! That is never going to happen."

He'd put his hands on my shoulders then and looked at me like he knew something. "Vinnie, I am serious. Promise me right now. You will move on and fall in love again, and our boys will have a father. I need to know that you will all be okay." He's looked at me with such seriousness, and I did promise him that day, but then I told him he would grow old with me, like we had planned.

There in the basement alone, that conversation felt like it came from a million years in the past, like the life we had known together was far, far away, and I felt sad knowing it would never be back.

The cleaning was done. I was about to go up the stairs from the basement. "I will always love you, Joey. I will keep my promise. I will move forward, even though I don't want to—and right now I can't imagine being able to. But I promised."

And then I promised myself, too, that I would take it moment by moment, that I would start to figure out what to do next, and at that moment it was simply to walk upstairs and face my world.

"Guess now who holds thee?"
"Death," I said. But there,
The silver answer rang,
"Not Death, but love."
—Elizabeth Barrett Browning

Part Two

Grief, Intuition, Healing

Telling Sal

JOEY AND I WERE MARRIED LESS THAN A YEAR WHEN HE AND I agreed that we were not going to have kids. We were having a good time and the thought of having a baby was not appealing. We had freedom, and a baby would be the end of that.

Some years later, Joey started to talk about having babies. I told him we could have a great life, that children would be hard work and would ruin the easy life we had. He knew I'd had a turbulent childhood. "It's not going to be your childhood all over again," he said. "You will not be alone. I'll be there with you. We'll be partners in this adventure, every step of the way." I believed him, and I knew we had so much love to give. Knowing he would be by my side made all the difference. In the summer of 1996, after we'd been living in our house for six months, we stopped using birth control and rolled the dice. I got pregnant immediately, but it ended in a miscarriage after eight weeks. Two years later, I gave birth to Sal. When Sal was nine months old I became pregnant with Vincent. Being parents was the hardest job we'd ever undertaken, but we were in it together, and I'd been so grateful that he was by my side.

Now Joey was gone, the three-week deadline had come, and Sal needed to know that his dad would not be coming home. I had to tell him in a quiet moment when the two of us were alone. I gave the boys all of my attention for the rest of the day, and I was so glad there was no quiet moment or opportunity for Sal and me to be alone. Why hurry to break his heart? I tried to enjoy every minute we had that day. I played with the boys, and when Sal and Vincent were laughing at something, I found myself wondering . . . How would I say it? What would I say? Sal was an innocent, happy little boy who knew the security of the love of both his mom and dad. That was about to end.

That evening after I got Vincent to sleep and Sal and I were alone, I could hold it off no longer. We were playing in the family room; I told Sal I had something to tell him.

"Okay, Mommy."

I sat down in front of him on the floor. He had been playing with his blocks. With no idea what to say, I heard myself: "Remember how we were praying that your dad would be coming home?"

"Yes, Mommy. My daddy will be coming home. You told me. I remember."

I remembered my dream and how real it had felt and how I had told Sal how Joey would be home soon. I cringed at the thought, and even though at that time I really believed it, I wished I had never said it.

I paused, gathering strength, then looked right into my little boy's eyes. "Sal, Daddy is not going to be able to come home. He died." His eyes looked into me and he started shaking his head. "No, Mommy, not my daddy!"

"Yes, Sal. I am so sorry, but your daddy did die."

He looked at me as though I had lost my mind and said, "Mommy, firefighters don't die."

"Sometimes they do."

With that he started crying and yelling, "No, not my daddy! Not my daddy!"

My stomach twisted and my heart pounded in my throat. As I held my arms out to him, he fell into my lap. I held his little body in my arms, and I started crying with him. His cry was loud and pained. His tiny soul was screaming. My body felt every vibration as he sobbed. At times he could not catch his breath. It was worse than all the waiting and not knowing. As I held Sal in my arms, the phone rang, and when I saw that it was Joan, I picked up. I really needed advice. Joan could hear Sal crying and moaning. It was the most terrible sound. I asked her what I could do to soothe him. She told me to do what I already knew to do: hold him. And I did, as he sobbed, but I wished she'd had a magical spell. As his mother I was supposed to protect him from any harm and pain. But every word that I had said cut into his innocence and brought him sorrow. His hero, his daddy, the big strong firefighter who nurtured and cared for him and made him feel safe and secure was dead. Sal's small world of his family was destroyed, just like that, and the person who was supposed to make it all better was now the person delivering the news. Nothing in my life hurt me more than that moment. Nothing.

As he cried I picked him up and brought him to my room. I put him on the bed and lay next to him and we both fell asleep. We slept for over eight hours. It was the first time I had slept through the night in three weeks. I woke when I heard Vincent calling me from the side of my bed. I pulled him into my arms and put him next to me. With Vincent in my arms, I watched Sal's sleeping face. He would be grieving his father, and it broke my heart, and then I looked at Vincent and realized that even though he did not understand and would not be grieving, he would never know his father. Joey wanted to teach them so much. Now they would never learn how to throw a baseball or football or learn to ski and snowboard from him. He would not be able to take them to ball games or teach them how to be men. They would never know the abundance of love that Joey had for them as they grew up. Joey and I had been together for twelve years, but our family of four had been together for less than two years.

Sal looked sad even as he slept. I waited until he woke to get out of bed. I did not want him to wake up alone. I did not know if he would cry again or how he would be feeling. When he woke, he acted as if nothing had happened the night before. He wanted to go in the family room and play. I thought that it was best to let him. He knew the truth now. Maybe he knew that there was nothing that he could do about it. I watched him play with his blocks, and I noticed a change in him. He was not calm and content like he usually was, but he did not seem sad either. He threw his blocks around and did not build things the way he always did. He was different, and there was nothing I could do about it. As a toddler, Sal's understanding of his loss was limited. How could he comprehend the ramifications of what I had told him the night before. He was not alone. I was thirty-four and I had no idea what our life was going to be like.

I was not expecting anyone to come over. I'd told Joan, when she brought the boys back from the beach the day before, that I had to start taking care of my family on my own. I was so afraid of being a single parent and living without Joey that I wanted to walk through the fear as quickly as possible. I had to face it.

Joan had said that many people in my situation still had a lot of people around them for help and support, but I still felt it was best to become independent as quickly as possible—like ripping off a Band-Aid®.

There is a time limit on how long people can help. I remembered when my father had died and how the neighbors had brought food to the house. It went on for about two weeks, and then one day, no more lasagna. Having had no control for the past three weeks, I needed to be in control of something. The only thing I could control right now was how I was going to deal with my loss.

This was my life, my mess; I had no choice. My mother could not be there for me because of her illness and because my grandmother needed her more. My in-laws saw things differently from the way that I did, and with Joey gone they were dealing with their own grief. Also, I was used to handling things on my own. When my mother was sick and my father was dying, I had to rely on myself. Not having support was familiar. In a strange way it was more comfortable for me to rely on myself than to ask for help. Past experiences had shown me that when I asked for help, it never came. The disappointment of that was more painful than the feeling of being left alone. But, I had never thought I would be in that place again. I had gotten accustomed to having a partner. And then it hit, like one more wave: The life I'd had with Joey was never coming back.

For three weeks, I had not really been there for the boys, so it was important to me that Sal and Vincent get all of my attention for at least one day. Yes, I felt sad and I had so many things that would need to be taken care of, but right now all that mattered was taking care of my boys.

Eggs

DOING THE SIMPLEST TASKS TOOK A MONUMENTAL EFFORT ON my part. It was morning. Sal was playing with his blocks. He said he was hungry. I told him I would make eggs. Luckily, two days earlier, my neighbor Joanne, had gone food shopping for me. She had been at the house helping with the boys, and she saw that the refrigerator was empty, so she made a list and drove to the store.

Ever since I had given birth to Sal, he had eaten only organic whole foods, but when I went to make the eggs that day, I discovered the eggs were not organic. I started to panic. I did not want to give them the eggs if they were not organic. I began to feel really stressed. I was not dressed, and I was exhausted, and I wanted to give the boys their breakfast. Suddenly all the variables were too much.

The phone rang. It was Joan calling to check up on us. I told her Sal had woken up, had wanted to play with his toys, and did not seem sad—but now I had a bigger problem: I did not have *organic* eggs. I kept repeating over and over again: "I don't have organic eggs, I don't know what to do, I don't have organic eggs, I don't know what to do, I don't have organic eggs, how am I going to make the fucking eggs . . ."

Joan tried to calm me down. "Okay, so the eggs are not organic," she said soothingly, "but the boys need to have breakfast. Make the scrambled eggs with the eggs you have."

Day one on my own and I am losing my mind. Should I get dressed? Should I dress the boys and go to Brooklyn, the nearest spot for organic eggs? My head was spinning. Sal had heard me on the phone with Joan and came into the room and as I was repeating, "I don't know what to do, I don't know what to do, I don't know what to do."

Sal came right over to me and stood staring up with his big, soft, brown eyes. "Just make the fucking eggs, Mommy."

Joan had heard him, too, and we both burst into laughter. Sal had never heard a foul word in his life, that was until Joey was missing. For three weeks I prayed in private, but when I did speak every other word out of my mouth had been "Fuck," and he'd learned well.

Sal's words were like a slap in my face and catapulted me immediately into action. I made the nonorganic scrambled eggs and the boys ate them. After the egg incident, I wanted to make sure that for the rest of the day the boys saw me as a bit more together. I owed it to them. There was so much on my mind: how was I going to deal with my grief, how would we live, how could I support us, how would I make the mortgage payments, what would we do for health benefits, how was I going to pay the bills that had mounted up over the past three weeks, and yet my one priority for this day was to make sure that both Sal and Vincent felt secure. I spent the rest of the day giving them all of my attention. I took them to play at the park. I bought them pizza for lunch—this was from money my neighbors had collected for us over the past few weeks—and I made them their favorite dinner, pasta, pecorino, and butter with broccoli. We played in the family room until it was time for bed and then I read them a bedtime story and let them sleep in my bed. During the whole day it felt as if both Sal and Vincent were clinging to me for dear life. I knew that Sal understood, but Vincent seemed to know, too, that I was all they had left. I did not mind that they slept in my bed with me. With his side of the bed empty, it felt like my life with Joey had never existed, but the boys were part of the life. They were real; they were proof of my life with Joey.

My body was so exhausted from the three weeks of no sleep that it wanted to shut down. Sleep became easier, and I was grateful for night.

With the morning came pain and worry: How will we live? How will I support us? I'll have to go back as a staff nurse. The boys and I will need benefits, so I won't be able to work per diem like I did when Joey was alive. I don't want to go back full time—the boys will need me. What if I go back as a part-time nurse? We could get benefits.

The mortgage, the mortgage, the mortgage. Could I finish the basement and make it into an apartment so rent would cover the payments? We lived on the beach block, and I knew how much I could get for an apartment steps to the beach. I could make the monthly payments that way.

We could live on my salary as a part-time nurse. I'd just have to be real careful with spending money, but I could put us on a tight budget. We were already living on a tight budget. I could make more money full-time, but I couldn't leave the boys. We wouldn't have a lot of money, but the boys and I would be together.

With each minute I knew how important it was to spend time with them. I could take money out of our small savings account to pay for materials to finish the basement, and I could ask the guys at the firehouse to help with the construction. Most of the guys, Joey included, had part-time jobs related to home improvement. They worked as plumbers, masons, painters, fence and window installers, so I knew they could help. I just had to ask them. I was grateful I could count on guys from the firehouse; I knew Joey would be the first one to help out a widow if he had lived. I thought about finances some more and was satisfied with the knowledge I'd be able to support us. We would have enough. I would see to that.

I'd had plenty of experience with not enough money. When I was a senior in high school my father suffered a massive heart attack. His heart was so damaged, he was on a list for a transplant. He couldn't walk across the room without shortness of breath, let alone work. Since there was no money coming in, I had three part-time jobs to help out. How scary it felt not knowing if we would be able to pay the bills and be able to keep our house. We watched every penny. That Christmas we could not afford presents or a tree, and things were so bad that we received a basket full of food from our church.

As a child I had collected cans and food every year for the poor at my church and school. I never thought that my family would ever be in need of it. We lived in a nice middle-class neighborhood, and in the past my father's salon was successful and we lived a comfortable life, but that was before he sold his salon and embarked on a business that ended in bankruptcy. He had been working two jobs and planning his next business move when he suffered the heart attack. So even though we were surrounded by money in our neighborhood, we just didn't have it anymore.

But that was just the beginning. A couple of months before he died, my father lost his mind and cancelled his life insurance policy. When I tried to help him after he dropped a glass, I received his last words: "Get the fuck away from me." I understood; I was used to dealing with my mother's mental illness.

After my father died, my mother really went downhill. Her fear of losing the house and fear of losing her job, when she had one, would always cause her to lose her mind. Eventually we went on public assistance and this was very humiliating for her. When she received food stamps she would shop in the next town because she was embarrassed that neighbors would see her. When she was well, my mother worked as a manicurist, but the fear of having to do acrylic nails, which she had no skills for, coupled with her fear of losing our home caused her so much stress that her mental health deteriorated and her manic symptoms of bipolar disorder resurfaced. She would get a job, she would get nervous about the job, then she would get scared and depressed, get manic, and get fired. This pattern repeated for years. I don't think there was a salon left on Long Island that my mother had not worked at and been fired from. In a sick way, it was comical.

I thought about my own situation: I was a widow and would no longer have Joey's income, but at least I had peace of mind knowing I would never suffer like my mother had, and I knew that Sal and Vincent would never have to go through what I had gone through. I was grateful to be in better shape than my mother had been. I had a Bachelor of Science degree, had graduated with honors, which gave me opportunities, and I had a profession. I knew that as a registered nurse I could make enough money to support us.

My mind was busy calculating: How much would it cost to build an apartment in the basement? Would the guys at the firehouse help? I hadn't been in touch with them since I had acknowledged that Joey had died, so part of the reason I was calling was to let them know that I now knew Joey had gone. I knew it would come as a relief to some of them. When I called, Richie answered the phone. I told him about how I was planning to go back on staff at the hospital so that we would have benefits, and he sounded shocked by my plan. "Vinnie, you will get Joey's benefits." He was surprised that I had not known this. Normally when a firefighter dies in the line of duty, the family is assigned a person from the FDNY who helps them with making funeral plans and informs them of the benefits they will receive, but because so many of the Staff Chiefs died that day, there was a breakdown in the system. Also there was a total of three hundred forty-three dead from the FDNY. It was hard for the Fire Department to reach out to all the families. Richie asked me if I wanted to speak to a widow from the firehouse whose husband died in a fire several years earlier. I remembered Joey telling me about this woman, as every December he went to her husband's memorial Mass at the church near the firehouse. She was the widow of our firehouse. In a million years I never thought I would talk to her, let alone be in the exact same position that she had been in years earlier. I hung up and waited for her to call me.

What could she possibly tell me? I was a little nervous as the phone rang, but she was very sensitive to me and told me how sorry she was about Joey. I thanked her, and I started telling her about how I was planning to support myself and the boys—"Honey," she said cutting me off, "I am sorry to tell you this but you are going to live better now than you did when your husband was alive." She meant that I would be better off financially. She explained to me that I would be receiving a pension and that I would be able to live off that alone, and that I could stay home and take care of my children. This idea of getting benefits was still so new to me—I was relieved, but it was not what I wanted, and she knew it. I wanted Joey. There was an understanding between the two of us like no one I had spoken with yet. She knew my sadness. She had lived through the loss of her own husband, and while she said the money was helpful, it would never replace a husband and father. She even knew the sadness that I would be facing in the future. I know she'd had children when her husband had died, so she'd already faced the challenges I would be meeting, and more importantly, she knew that our lives would never be the same. It was like she was welcoming me into a club that neither of us wanted to be a part of, and I could feel that she was sad that I was now a member.

When I hung up the phone there was a battle going on. One side of my head was screaming, "I don't fucking want this!" The other side, "Honey, I am sorry to tell you this, but you will live better now"—'round and 'round in a loop; it felt so wrong. I wanted my life with Joey, not this. But I was relieved to hear that I would at least be allowed to grieve without worry. I was relieved the boys and I would be okay financially.

Money Can't Buy Me . . .

EARLY IN OCTOBER, A NEIGHBOR OFFERED TO TAKE ME DOWN
to a pier in Manhattan where the city had set up an information
and financial assistance station for the victims' families affected
by 9/11. Representatives from the Social Security office, the City of
New York, the FDNY, and other government agencies were there,
as well as people who volunteered their time, such as massage
therapists, Reiki masters, grief counselors, trauma therapists,
social workers, as well as charities of all kinds including the Red
Cross and Salvation Army.

When we got inside, it was very crowded. The place was packed
with people on lines, and there were tables and tables with the
names of different organizations draped with banners. I had never
seen anything like it. Immediately, I was taken to a table to help
the family members of the FDNY. There, I was assigned to a fire
department member who escorted me around to the different
tables. I was so grateful there was someone to help me, because the
place was overwhelming, noisy, and confusing. I was told there were
organizations that wanted to help the victims' families financially
and that I had to be there to talk with them because they wanted to
make sure the funds went directly to the family members. At each
table I had to tell them my name and the name of my next of kin

who had died at the World Trade Center. All I had to do was say Joey's name and what my relationship to him was and I got checks. It was strange to me that there were so many organizations there all wanting to help the families. Since I was so caught up in praying for Joey's safe return, I had not realized how much of an impact the attacks had had on people. This event seemed to touch so many people in our country, as well as people from around the world. It seemed that with the outpouring of grief came an abundance. People wanted to donate to show they cared.

I was getting dizzy going from table to table. Thank goodness for the fire department escort. I was still in shock, so it was hard to keep track of where I was and where I was going in the sea of people and tables. As I walked around the large space, and checks were being handed to me by every organization, a part of me wanted to run away. I understood what was going on, and I could appreciate the sentiments behind the kind gestures, but there were not enough checks in the world to make up for losing Joey. I kept fantasizing that Joey would come running through the doors calling my name with his arms open, and I could drop the checks on the ground and run into his arms and we could go back to living our happy, simple life.

For the most part, the pier was set up to give financial aid, but it was also necessary that official documents be filed. The City of New York had a table just to file death certificates, and the Social Security Administration also had a table so papers could be filed. When they handed me Joey's death certificate, I looked at the cause of death: Homicide. My head swirled. MURDER? Thank God, I was sitting, because I think my legs would have given out if I had been standing. I had never thought of Joey's death as a murder. Holding a death certificate made me feel like my life with Joey was so far away. Nothing made sense. I held an envelope full of checks, instead of having a life with my husband, and I was holding a death certificate as proof that my life would never be the same.

I'd had enough. It was an outpouring of generosity, but I was exhausted and ready to leave. I was heading for the exit when I was stopped by a volunteer. She must have seen on my face the struggle I had gone through in the past weeks. I guess my face like many people's there that day told a story. She suggested I have a massage and a Reiki session. My neighbor told me that I should, so I decided to go. My body was aching, and I had lost the ability to relax, so I accepted her offer.

At first my mind and body raced. Shallow breath, heart pounding. But a few minutes into the session, I became very relaxed. The Reiki masters never touched me directly. They just waved their hands very close over my body, and it was very relaxing. It was the most calm I had felt in a month. I had never had a Reiki session before, but I understood the principles. It was about balancing the energy in my body and mind, and not only did it make sense to me, it was working. It was like I had taken a drug. My body was able to slow down, and my mind felt clearer.

After my session, I received a massage for a half hour. It was the first time I had been touched by another human being in a long time, and I felt comforted. As a nurse, I knew about studies done on babies who were not held or nurtured after birth, just fed and changed, but not really touched. They often did not gain weight, or grow well. Babies in this situation were labeled as "failure to thrive," and most died. I understood now more than ever the benefits of affection and touch. I felt how much my body was starved for nurturing. Joey had always been affectionate, and I realized how much I was missing his touch, hugs, and affection. I knew with the touch of the massage therapist that if I was going to survive without Joey, I would need to seek natural ways to heal my mind and body.

It had been a long day, and I felt grateful to my neighbor for taking me to the pier, and for insisting I take advantage of the services that were so generously given. We were about to leave when I was offered an opportunity to go to Ground Zero. Once before, I had been invited to go and see it by the fire department, but I'd turned it down. I'd had no interest; after all, I knew Joey was alive so why shake my faith?

I was about to turn down this new offer when my neighbor told me that someday I might regret not going. I thought about it; he was sincere, and he said that he would go with me. The only way down there was by ferry—the roads to Ground Zero were all closed due to debris—so we would be going via the Hudson River.

I was a little disoriented when we got on the boat and headed down the west side of Manhattan. This was not an area I was familiar with. I had no idea how long it would take to get the there and was surprised it took only minutes. As the boat pulled into the dock, it was hard to know where we were. It was only when we got out and walked a couple of blocks that we could see the torn and twisted remains of the Towers. There was smoke from the smoldering site, and it was misty. As I walked through the path they had cleared in the debris, I was struck by how familiar it was. I felt like I had seen or experienced it before. An eeriness came over me. My mind couldn't make any sense of what I was feeling. It was only later that I realized the site was the same as the dream that shook me to my core and left me with dread that something horrible was about to happen to Joey. In that dream, amongst the white clouds of smoke I could see giant jagged steel cutting through the haze, exactly like the top of the mountain peak in my dream, and the same eerie feeling was present.

We walked closer to the site and a woman behind me fainted when she saw the twisted smoldering steel. As she went down her family member caught and picked her up and she came to only to start sobbing. I was unable to feel, yet knew her grief. Still, I remained numb. I had no emotional attachment to the site. It only represented where Joey died, not where he lived.

My sadness lived at home, where there was an empty space and signs of his life I could not escape. There was the closet with his clothes. His side of the bed. His place at the table. His razor was in our medicine cabinet. His toothbrush still in the cup next to mine, and his bicycle and helmet in our basement. Everything was still there waiting for him.

Since accepting Joey's death, I had never focused on his remains, but chose to concentrate on his spirit. Looking around I knew that it was only by chance that anyone could have survived this. It felt like death. As I stood there taking it all in, I was aware why Joey's colleagues knew he couldn't have survived that day, and I understood why they were confused by my belief that he would come home. I knew his body was there, but I felt he had long gone from this place where his life ended. I felt his soul was free from his body and his spirit was with the boys and me. This belief helped me cope with what I was witnessing. I had only been to the World Trade Center once a couple of years before, but I knew how impressive the site had been. What I saw now looked like a war-ravaged city. The air was thick and had a strange acrid odor that mixed with the smell of the smoke.

As I walked away and got back on the boat, I looked back. I could hardly believe that Joey's last moments of life had been here. It had no place in our lives. I would remember him instead smiling from our front door that morning telling me he loved me. I would remember how he lived. That is all I would allow into my heart. I looked behind the boat as it moved away from the pier and watched the wake form. When I gazed up, I saw how quickly Ground Zero disappeared in the distance, and I felt good as it grew smaller and smaller, because I would never allow it to be part of my memories of Joey, or my life.

The Memorial

IT WAS THE DAY I GOT HOME FROM THE PIER THAT I STARTED planning Joey's memorial. I chose his birthday which was October tenth. I wanted to celebrate his life and not focus so much on his death. My in-laws did not understand this approach; they saw Joey as gone and rotting somewhere. I felt he was in a better place. I could not prove this to them, but I still felt a connection and knew he was okay.

I planned the memorial with the help of neighbors, our church, and the FDNY. My neighbor Mary helped me pick out prayers and music, and my neighbor Joanne made a collage of various pictures of Joey that would be placed at the front of the altar. She also enlarged one of my pictures of him and had it framed for the altar of the church. The church had had more than its share of experience with memorials after September eleventh. There were too many firefighters and business professionals from our area who had been killed. Joey's memorial was one of many that Saint Francis de Sales held. It became all too common to see a memorial fire truck and thousands of off-duty firefighters in the neighborhood standing outside the church. There were private memorials as well, at least once or twice a week, for many weeks. There were also some funerals in the cases where bodies were recovered. All the help and support

I received made the task of planning the memorial somewhat effortless, and I prayed the actual day would go as easily.

An hour before the start of the memorial my in-laws showed up at my house with some other family members. This was unexpected. I had planned to meet them at the church. After the service, I would talk with them at the restaurant where I was providing lunch to members of Joey's firehouse, our friends, and their families. I invited them in, but the timing was not good. My two boxers, who were already on edge, were now in the backyard barking at the voices coming from inside the house. I was trying to dress the boys and explain a little bit to Sal about why we were going to church. I needed peace and privacy. Instead, I was dealing with a house full of people. I felt choked up and very claustrophobic, and since I was not going to have time alone in my home, I left the house for a few moments and walked to the beach. I thought it best for the boys to stay at the house, since I was feeling an array of negative emotions, and I did not want the boys to feel my tension. When I got to the beach I felt like I could breathe. I stood there watching the repetitive waves crashing and started to feel some calm.

I was there only a few minutes when I heard a familiar voice: "Hi, they said you would be here." I had forgotten Joan was coming over to help with the boys, and I was so grateful to see her. Her solid friendship allowed me to cry. "My house is full of people when I need to be alone with my boys; I told my mother-in-law the plan was to meet at the church, I'm not sure she gets the details, she's too grief stricken—"

"Okay," she murmured.

With Joey's death, I had gained the added the responsibility of dealing with my in-laws' raw emotions. With all I had on my plate it was just too much—there was too much to handle, to take in, and

I was just starting to comprehend it all, and in minutes I had to go face the world and a public acknowledgment of Joey's death.

Joan's sympathetic words and loving support helped so much. Just venting my frustrations helped. I had no control over what the day would be, but I did have control over my feelings, and I had already made up my mind to hold in my emotions. I did not want to scare my sons by losing control and sobbing. I thought of Jacqueline Kennedy and of how composed she was at her husband's funeral. I had decided I would carry myself in the same way she had. My feelings were private, just as my life with Joey had been, and I would keep it that way. Joan and I walked back to the house together. I felt like I could handle now whatever the day would bring.

As Joan and the boys and I got to the limousine and pulled away from my street, I saw a sight that brought tears to my eyes. There were crowds and crowds of people. Hundreds of firefighters lined up and down Rockaway Beach Boulevard. News vans and reporters outside the church, and hundreds more people. I was deeply moved to see how many firefighters were there. Joey's was not the only fire department memorial that day. I knew of several others scheduled all around New York. The newspapers printed lists. I was shocked as well as grateful to see so many members of the FDNY lined up for Joey.

Joey had never missed a funeral. On one occasion, he had gone with a fever and the flu. Nothing would stop him from honoring a fellow brother, and I felt it was karma that all these firefighters and fire officers were there to honor him. I almost lost my ability to control my tears when I saw all of them in their navy suits. I remembered how handsome Joey had looked in his suit, and how proud I always was of him. He truly deserved this turnout.

When I stepped out of the limo, I saw familiar faces. No tears, no tears. There were Joey's friends that he had grown up with and all the people he had invited to our wedding. I saw nurses and other staff with whom I had worked at the hospital, neighbors from our block and from where we had lived in our apartment in Brooklyn, neighbors from my childhood, friends and coworkers from all our jobs in the past. I was touched; it was so much to take in. Inside the church, I could see that all the seats were taken and there were rows and rows of people standing in the back and on the sides. I had heard that Mayor Giuliani would be there. Former Governor Hugh Carey of New York State was there, as well as the chief of the fire department. We settled into our front row seats and my mind flashed back to the last firefighter funeral I had attended with Joey.

We were standing outside the church. It was one of the "Father's Day" funerals that had claimed the lives of three firefighters. There were so many people that they'd put audio speakers outdoors so people could hear what was happening inside the church. I remembered Mayor Giuliani addressing the widow of the firefighter and speaking of the sacrifice her husband made. "I never want to be that woman sitting there," I'd said to Joey. I had felt so sorry for her and her sons and so grateful that Joey had been standing next to me. I remembered the gratitude I felt for the life we had, and how Joey had told me he never wanted me to be that woman either. Later when he brought it up at home, I said the same thing I always did when he tried to get me to promise that I'd move on: "Never! If anything happened to me, I'd haunt any woman you married." But, he had not been in the mood for jokes that night.

Even in my dreams I only could see myself with Joey. I'd had dreams where I was a teenager again. Joey and I didn't know each other yet, but every time the man in the dream asked me out or tried to kiss me, I would say, "No, I can't, because I love Joey." It became a joke between us. I could never see myself in life or even in my dreams with any other man, and he knew this about me. So the night after that funeral of his firefighter colleague, it had been important to him that I promise to go on and love another man if he were to die. Deep down inside, I had known it could happen, but I did not want to face it, and that night I had not wanted a serious conversation. Instead, I just kept trying to joke. "Am I allowed to mourn you?" I asked. "I'll give you one year," he answered, "but then I'm going to come down and kick your ass if you haven't moved on." I told him he had a deal. But when I laughed and said it would never happen, Joey didn't smile.

Now I was "that woman."

I was sitting next to my mother-in-law. Joan was behind me with the boys. My mother, her boyfriend, and my brother were in the next row. It was quiet and somber. But as the priest prepared to begin, my mother-in-law saw the picture of Joey at the center of the church and she screamed and hiccuped into sobs. Instantly, Joey's relatives formed a line where we were sitting. They started kissing and hugging my mother-in-law. Some who knew who I was, hugged me as well. The priest saw he was not going to be able to control the line of Italian relatives who were trying to comfort my mother-in-law, so he waited, but with each passing relative her screaming grew louder. Sal grew frightened, so Joan tapped me on the shoulder and told me she would take him out for little while. In the meantime, as the crowd waited, I found myself flanked by Joey's well-intentioned relatives who seemed to be looking at me oddly—because I was not crying, or screaming, or wearing black? I do not know. The louder my mother-in-law screamed, the more her family queued for her. I thought that the priest would never gain control over the service or

Joey's family. Finally he got the message across to them that he was going to start, and the relatives found their seats.

After he finished, he introduced Mayor Giuliani, and Joan, who was still outside, heard the clapping and brought Sal back in, walking him to the front of the church, whispering, "They are clapping for you, baby." Sal smiled at me, and I was relieved he had been calmed.

As the Mayor spoke, my mother-in-law continued to cry and scream. I knew that in her family tradition this was common practice. Yes, she was hurting, but the fact was, it was hard to hear what was being said to honor Joey.

My sons were directly behind me, and I knew they would be looking to me for cues. They would have been confused and upset if I had cried. So I didn't. My mother-in-law and I sat side-by-side, but we couldn't have been more different. Everything about how we viewed Joey's life and death was different. The only thing we had in common was that we both loved him deeply and both of our hearts were broken. One would think that simple truth would have created a tight bond, but it seemed to almost make our relationship worse. I felt isolated from her. There had been no sense of order since Joey died; he was no longer there to balance out the personal differences, and her loud screaming and crying told me that not only was she unable to cope with her own grief, she was not going to be there for my boys, or me.

When the service ended and while we were lined up outside for the Honor Guard of the fire department to play their bagpipes and perform their traditional salute, and while the news cameras rolled and the photographers snapped away with their cameras, my mother-in-law started to scream and cry again. Suddenly, I felt very tired. I wanted to run and hide, but instead I stood. The day was not about me. It was about honoring Joey, and I felt such gratitude that so many people had shown up to pay their respects to him. I was proud of him. I was proud of the fact that he never looked for recognition.

Our New Life

A COUPLE OF MONTHS AFTER JOEY'S MEMORIAL, I RECEIVED a call from the firehouse. I was asked to clean out his locker and retrieve his car. It had to be done. The Honda had been parked there since he had shown up for work that last morning. New guys had been hired and they needed his locker. Going to Joey's locker and taking his things home, though, was a reminder that my life was never going to be the same.

I didn't really need reminders. Sal had changed dramatically. He had always been such a happy little toddler and now he was confused and too young to understand or express it. When I had to go to the dentist for a toothache, I brought both boys with me, and when the dental assistant who had spoken so highly of Sal on September tenth said hello to him, he kicked her. The change in him was also evident at home. I was cleaning in the kitchen and the boys were in the family room. There were no walls between the two rooms so I could always keep my eyes on them. I had to use the bathroom so I checked on the boys first. I was cautious about leaving them alone after an incident earlier in the week where Sal had destroyed our china closet door by stripping the lattice woodwork off of it. He never did things like that. Even when he was a year and a half he was respectful of our home. For Sal to be ripping things apart was a clear indication he was struggling, so I knew I had to be mindful.

Before I went to the bathroom, I saw that Sal was putting basketballs through a little plastic hoop that was suctioned to the wall, and Vincent was playing with blocks; it was safe to leave them for a few minutes. I was in the bathroom for only a minute when I heard Vincent crying. From the bathroom I saw Sal shaking his basketball hoop back and forth around Vincent's neck. "Stop!" I yelled, shocked by Sal's violence. He seemed to be oblivious to Vincent's cries and suffering. It was like Sal was possessed with rage. I ran into the room and cried out for him to stop but it was like he didn't hear me. "Stop!" I yelled. But he didn't. The more Sal shook the hoop, the harder Vincent cried. Out of control myself, I took the hoop off Vincent and I put it over Sal's head and I started to shake him, the way he had been shaking Vincent. I wanted Sal to feel what Vincent was feeling. As I shook him he started to cry. I stopped shaking the hoop and dropped it. "What the hell am I doing? What kind of animal have I become?" I was horrified at what I had just done, and I felt so sad. I no longer recognized who I was. I had always been calm and happy and full of love toward the boys. Where had I gone? My nerves were raw. I was incapable of seeing straight. The boys were both crying. I looked into their eyes and I could see their fear and pain. They were only babies and had never experienced anything like this before, so they were frightened. As I came to my senses I knelt down and put my arms around both of them and hugged and kissed them and told them how sorry I was. We were all sobbing. No reassuring words from me could stop them from crying, and when their tears eventually did stop, I could see that neither was consoled. Whether it was the reality or just my perception, I now felt like they had lost confidence in me as a mother. I believed the boys were looking at me and thinking: So this is it? You are our sole caretaker? God help us.

I knew this was a cry from Sal for help, but I was hanging on by a thread. How could I help Sal heal when I was devastated?

The next thing I knew, I was screaming at God, "Are you fucking kidding me? My husband, the father to my children is dead. I can't recognize Sal. He's in pain. I'm full of heartache. I can barely get out of bed in the morning, and now I am supposed to deal with this, on my own? How I am supposed to cope with this? Where is my back-up? Help me!"

I needed Joey like I had never needed him before. Despair turned to anger, and rage flashed. Before I knew what I was doing, I had grabbed one of our kitchen chairs and thrown it across the room. I wanted that chair in bits. As it hit the ground, it did not break. Instead, it bounced, and that enraged me even more. How dare it still be whole! I picked it up and started pounding it on the floor until it was in pieces. I thought I'd feel good seeing it lying in bits, but I didn't; I was even more pained, and now I had a broken chair. I crumbled to the ground and sobbed. The room was stone quiet, except for my crying. I realized the boys were staring at me in shock. I couldn't take it anymore. I wanted to run away, but I had the boys. I was overwhelmed, but they were my life.

At some point, my mind focused on a sound: the boys' soft whimpers. I dropped the piece of wood I still held and hurried over to them, hugged them, and now I was crying as I told them how sorry I was.

Something was seriously wrong with me, and I grew frightened. I needed help, but the only person I could call was Joan, and I felt I had exhausted her. I was desperate. I needed professional help. I had to act. I composed myself enough to get on the phone to Joey's firehouse. I knew there would be support for me there. I didn't quite know how they would help, but I just knew that this was my lifeline. Tony picked up the phone, and I thanked God that he'd answered. He'd done the eulogy at Joey's memorial and had been a great support to me. I told him that I thought there was something mentally wrong with me and explained what had happened and how I felt like I was losing my mind.

He couldn't have been nicer. "It's okay," he said. "Give yourself a break." Those simple words made me feel like less of monster for having behaved the way I did. He told me there would be someone right there for me. He said he'd lost it plenty of times with his own children and he'd never gone through what I had been through. This didn't really reassure me. What had happened was not normal; it was insanity. I should never have acted like that.

The longer I spoke with Tony the more I started to feel like myself. He told me to relax until someone got there.

As I hung up the phone, my immediate attention was drawn to the broken chair. Now I just wanted it gone. It was a scary reminder of the madness that had just happened. After cleaning up all the pieces and putting them in a box in the basement for no one to ever see, including myself, I sat down with the boys to give them some reassurance. There was now a tentative calm in the room. We all sat on the couch. I read a book to the boys and then I watched them play. Things appeared normal.

The doorbell rang and the dogs in the yard started barking. It had been an hour since I had called the fire department, and now Tony and a social worker were at my doorstep. I felt relieved the minute they walked through the door. My prayers were finally answered, or maybe I had shocked God into action.

The social worker explained that I was going through Post-Traumatic Stress, PTS. This shocked me. I thought this related to Vietnam veterans, or people directly related to a trauma, not realizing that I qualified. I was convinced I was losing my mind, and it was a huge relief for me to know that there was a reason for my behavior, even though I could never excuse it. She recommended I see a therapist for a while.

Tony and the social worker left. I felt hopeful. I made an appointment that week with a therapist. I knew that if I was going to pick up the pieces of my life I had to start treating myself like I would one of my patients in the hospital.

$$\infty$$

Our two boxers, Chelsea and Durante, continued to wait for Joey. I did whatever I could to ease their pain. I gave the Honda to Joey's brother. If the dogs heard its engine they would expect Joey to walk in the door. It would have been too cruel to have them excited just to be disappointed. I wished that I could have had a way to explain to the dogs that Joey had not abandoned them. They looked for him every day. In the evening they would wait near the door at the time Joey would arrive home. Most nights they would wait by the door for hours. After I put the boys to sleep, I would have to go to the door and coax them to their beds. Every night it was the same. It broke my heart to see them there. They missed him. They loved him, and now he was gone and they had no way to understand.

One morning I attempted to walk the dogs with the boys. I held Vincent in my arms, had the two leashes in one hand, and held Sal's hand in my other. I ran into a neighbor who used to talk to Joey when he walked the dogs. He asked how we were doing and then asked about the dogs. "They miss Joey, and their long morning walks—they're really struggling without him."

"I'm free in the mornings," he said. "I could walk them."

What a gift his words were! I happily accepted his offer. He agreed to walk them every morning and told me that he could be at my house at eight a.m. The next morning he arrived right on time. I was a little embarrassed because the boys and I were still in our pajamas. I had always been an early riser and was really organized with the kids, but that had changed. I put Chelsea and Durante's collars on and handed him the leashes. The dogs needed time and attention; they seemed so lost without their beloved Joey. While they were gone, I planned to get the house in order and get the boys and myself dressed. I started to clean up the kitchen, but emptying the dishwasher became a challenge. I would hold a plate in my hand and forget what I was doing. I was not even aware of time anymore. It took me almost a half hour to empty it.

When the doorbell rang, I was still in my pajamas. My neighbor said he had been gone over two hours. "I thought you'd be dressed now." He paused, looked down, then met my eyes. "Did you ever think about putting the boys in daycare?"

I hardly knew what to say. I didn't like daycare and didn't trust it, but he told me about a woman who ran a daycare right in our neighborhood. "She's a friend, and I trust her. Both of my kids go there. They get to play with other kids, and they really like it."

When he left, I started to think about what was best for the boys and for me. Six weeks earlier I would never have entertained the thought of daycare when I was at home. Joey and I had been the boys' sole caregivers; we arranged our workdays around them. When I worked, Joey cared for them, and when he worked, I cared for them. That was our routine. To be contemplating putting the boys into daycare tore me apart, but suddenly as I stood there in my pajamas, losing my mind, with my house in disarray and the boys needing something I could no longer give them, daycare seemed like a good option.

The first morning I took them, I was terrified. When I got there the boys seemed so happy they ran straight to the toy box. The place was lovely—filled with life, color, crafts, and wonderful toys. I immediately had a good feeling and felt comfortable at the thought of leaving Sal and Vincent, but when I got up to leave, both boys went hysterical. "Don't leave, Mommy!" Sal was so distressed, and my heart was breaking. It felt unnatural to leave them. The woman reassured me this was normal, but as I held tears back I felt that this was anything but normal for me. Still, I walked toward the door, opened it, and left. As the door closed behind me and I heard my sweet boys crying inside, I completely lost it. Weeping, I walked the two blocks to my house and immediately called the woman to see how they were. I had made up my mind if they were still crying I would go back and get them. She told me they were fine and I didn't hear crying in the background.

I hung up the phone, walked straight into my bedroom, and collapsed on my bed. I was now free to do exactly what I wanted, and that was to lie there and cry. I was no longer a nurse, a wife, a happy mother. All gone. The fear of upsetting the boys was gone too. Exhausted, I cried myself to sleep, slept a few hours, and woke with a bit of my burden lifted.

In the afternoon, I returned to pick up the boys, better able to cope with them. As painful as leaving them was, I realized that I needed time alone to heal, and in turn help them heal. The first few days were the hardest on the boys, but then it became part of their routine, and mine, from Monday to Friday.

Since my new focus in life was healing, and since I did not want to burden anyone for help, I hired a babysitter/housekeeper who helped me with the chores and with the boys in the afternoon. If I needed to run out of the house to get diapers, I did not have to pack up the boys in their car seats. I now had someone there to back me up. It was great having help with the housework, too. I was no longer able to multitask, and I had little energy to do even the easiest of responsibilities. My brain had been fried. I no longer got joy out of the things that I used to love. I had no appetite, and if I cooked a dinner for the boys, they were not interested in eating it. We had always eaten heartily as a family of four. Now it was like we all had attention deficit disorder: they could not sit down and eat a whole dinner, and I had no desire or energy to cook one. Oh, I cooked small meals. I made mac and cheese for the boys, and pasta, but my days of three course meals from scratch were gone. Without Joey there to enjoy them, the effort was pointless.

Having someone there to help, then, was the best decision I could have made. I needed someone to come in and take care of things the way I once had. I remembered one of the last big meals I'd cooked, one we'd shared as a family. It was September ninth. I had worked the seven a.m. to three p.m. shift that day. I drove home with the windows open and the radio turned up. I couldn't wait to strip out of my nursing uniform and slip into shorts and a T-shirt and see my family. It was a perfect day, no humidity, warm and sunny. As I reached my street, I felt a surge of happiness, as I always did when I was almost home. I loved our little house by the beach and our life there.

Our van was parked in front, so I pulled the Honda into the back parking spot and entered the house through the back door. We never locked our doors. With Chelsea and Durante there, it was like having security guards. I walked into the kitchen and was greeted by wagging tails and licks. I loved the reception they gave me, I loved them like I loved the boys.

Around the house there was evidence of where Joey and the boys had been and what they were doing. Although I missed them and wanted to see them, I was relieved to find the house empty and grateful for a little solitude. This break gave me time to tidy their mess. I loved our home orderly and prided myself on the ability to straighten and clean up quickly. I raced to change my clothes, then walked around barefoot as I threw in a load of laundry and folded and put away what was in the dryer. I picked up toys, put them away, quickly vacuumed, and was satisfied that the house was organized and clean. Since it seemed I had time to spare, I decided to cook dinner. When the gang got back from the beach, I would be ready for them. I loved taking care of them. I loved to cook; it was a way to show my love and to nurture my family. Everything was organic, balanced, and healthy. I cooked from scratch; we never ate anything processed. At that very moment, I was feeling very satisfied with myself—I was amazing! I got up at five, left the house at six, worked all day, cleaned the house, and now I had made dinner. I could do it all! How lucky Joey was to be married to me. A song came to mind from a 1970s commercial, and I laughed to myself as I cooked. "I can bring home the bacon and fry it up in a pan and never ever let you forget you're a man, cause I'm a woman." I was a career woman, wife, and mother. Was there anything I couldn't do?

My life was perfect. There was nowhere else I would rather be, and I wanted for nothing—although I did dream of a kitchen with actual countertops. The kitchen was a decent size, but there was not enough counter space. I became very creative in my quest for space and would often use a plastic cutting board on top of our oven, although once or twice I almost started a fire by forgetting to take the chopping board off before I preheated the oven. I even melted part of a boom box once that I left on the stove.

Someday I would have a proper kitchen. It was a dream, something to look forward to, not something that was missing. I was living a dream: I had a wonderful man, two healthy sons, and a career that I loved. We were living our "happily ever after." Oh sure, we had our moments like every married couple, but they were always worked through and ultimately added to the marriage and made it stronger and better. Any obstacles that came up were met with respect; we had great ability to work things out together. We were not the same in a lot of ways, but that was where the attraction came from. The chemistry and magic never left, even after almost twelve years. The life I was living was like the fantasy I had dreamed as a little girl—I always felt like I was playing house.

I cooked dinner and put it in the oven to keep it warm. It was still so beautiful out. I quickly fed the dogs and decided to walk them down to the beach so I could see my guys. I was full pride as I walked. Wait until Joey sees me. He'll be so happy—and then I'll tell him that dinner is ready and all he has to do is take a shower. I've taken care of everything—he'll feel so grateful that he has me. He'll be thinking: She worked all day and cooked and cleaned the house. He'll think he's married to a superwoman! I pictured his smiling face full of pure love and admiration.

It was perfect timing. Here he came walking toward me pulling the boys in our wagon, a picture of domestic bliss, but as I drew closer I registered his grim expression.

"What the hell happened to you? Where are our snacks?"

"Snacks? I made dinner. It's all on the table." I flashed him my biggest smile.

"Didn't you see the note?"

"What note?"

He straightened up and glared at me. "The note on the refrigerator that said, 'We are at the beach, please bring snacks.'"

Since I had gone in the back door, I had not seen the refrigerator directly upon entering, but I had been in and out of it several times while cooking—uh oh, superwoman had a flaw. "Sorry." I knew better than to get mad; I knew how he was wired. He was like a bear when hungry and tired. I explained. Still, he wasn't impressed with my superwoman feats. He was too pissed and too hungry. I tried to hide my amusement. He could always make me laugh, even when he was angry. He reminded me of Donald Duck. As we trudged together back to the house, I just let him rant on about how I'd missed the note. I knew his testiness would pass the minute he put one bite of my chicken cutlets in his mouth. All I had to do was get food into him and then my lovable man would be back. He still wore his pissed look in the shower and mumbled a couple of times to himself and shook his head once or twice, all of which I ignored.

When we sat down and that first forkful of chicken cutlet passed his lips, his sense of humor miraculously returned—as predicted. Now, he was laughing at himself and at me. After dinner he loaded the dishwasher and I cleaned the table.

It was still so beautiful out that I wanted to go for a bike ride, but Joey did not want to go. He was worried about our safety; the sun was starting to set. I told him how cooped up I had felt all day at work and reminded him we'd hardly broken in Vince's bike seat. He agreed then, but insisted on a route different than our usual one— one he thought was safer. It was on the boardwalk. We would take the boys to the playground.

I had Vincent on my bike and Sal rode on Joey's. We were literally riding into the sunset. I remember thinking it was like a picture, the final scene of a movie. We ran into a detour where they were repairing the boardwalk. Joey made sure our path was safe as we rode near to the cars and traffic. He kept looking back to make sure Vincent and I were close behind. When we got back on the boardwalk the boys waved to each other, as Joey and I raced, smiles on their little faces. At the playground they ran around chasing each other. As they came across a small bridge, Joey pretended to be a monster and grabbed at their feet. They giggled and ran past him crying out, "You can't get me, bad monster."

I watched the boys giggling and Joey doing his best monster voice, then gazed up at the expansive sky stretching toward Manhattan. In the background, waves crashed on the beach. I turned toward Joey. "We are the luckiest people in the world." He beamed. Behind him the sky was turning a deep shade of magenta.

I cannot recall a more beautiful evening at our home on the Atlantic than that last time we rode bikes together, with our two smiling, happy children. I now know how precious that night was, because it would be the very last time we would ride together, ever.

Kelly

SHORTLY AFTER VINCENT WAS BORN, I WAS DIAGNOSED WITH hypothyroidism. Since I was working three days a week and also taking care of the boys, my doctor suggested I take time out of my day to rest. We needed a babysitter.

Kelly was thirteen and lived across the street; but she was not a typical teenager. She was an old soul—much wiser than her years—smart, with an amazing sense of humor. Joey and I got a kick out of just how sharp she was. We both loved the way she interacted with Sal and Vincent. I had hired her so that I could have an hour to myself during the day to rest and relax. I could take a walk on the beach or take a nap while she played with the boys, and she was the first person we called to babysit when we went out.

After 9/11, Kelly came over so much that she became a member of the family. In the evenings, after she did her homework, she would walk across the street and give me a hand, whether it was helping the boys with their baths and getting them dressed for bed or entertaining them as I cleaned up after dinner. Kelly treated the boys as I did; she was like an extension of me. She knew their personalities, never let them get away with bad behavior, and they loved her. For me, Kelly was a true friend. Even with twenty years between us, I was as close to Kelly as I was with friends my own age. Even as a teenager, she understood my loss. She had known Joey well and had witnessed our relationship. She knew I had lost someone special.

Being young, she also knew a lot about technology. Kelly taught me how to use my computer and how to download music. We downloaded old disco songs and danced around the house. Our favorite artist was Barry White. We danced to "Can't Get Enough of Your Love," over and over. The boys danced with us. Acting silly and dancing always raised our moods. Then, after all of the dancing, we would sit and relax and listen to music. One of my favorite songs, Fleetwood Mac's "Landslide," seemed like an anthem for me. Kelly and I sang it so much that Vincent had memorized it too.

Kelly's wisdom, honesty, and friendship kept me afloat.

The Cruise to Nowhere

BY LATE OCTOBER, I WAS STARTING TO REALLY FEEL THE IMPACT of Joey's death. I woke every day to emptiness. As a family, we were like a puzzle missing a piece, and I had no idea how to complete it. I was doing my best to create a life, but no matter how busy and productive I tried to be, I longed for Joey's company and support.

Every day was the same: me alone with the boys with no one there to catch us if we fell. The weekends were particularly hard, because I was alone with the boys morning, noon, and night with no breaks or adult company. It was not that I did not enjoy the boys' company, but how much block playing and Thomas the Train can a person take? I longed for adult conversation, even for just a few minutes. If the boys and I were invited to go anywhere on the weekend and I had the chance to be around adults, we went. So, in early November when a free trip came up for a weekend, one would have thought that I would have jumped at the chance to go. The opposite was true. A major cruise line was launching a new giant ship and wanted to give something back to the Fire Department for all their efforts during and after 9/11. The ship was set to sail from Manhattan to somewhere out in the Atlantic and then just turn around and come back. It was officially dubbed The Cruise to Nowhere.

Initially, when the guys from Joey's firehouse told me about it, I declined the invitation. The idea of going on a getaway without Joey was too painful. Also traveling alone with two toddlers seemed too hard a task. I never gave it a second thought until one afternoon in early November when I went for a haircut. The woman who cut my hair was the wife of one of the firefighters from Joey's firehouse. After 9/11 I found myself in her chair often. I liked the way she did my hair, but really I went for the company. She was happily married and knew what I had lost. She was supportive as well as compassionate.

That afternoon she was telling me she was going on the cruise, and that I should go too. "You could use the break, Vinnie. I'll be there to help. So will the other families. They have a spa on the ship and childcare. You could pamper yourself and the boys would have fun." I explained that traveling on my own with the boys was not my idea of a break. She kept saying that everyone wanted to help me.

So I started to think about it. It would be nice to have support. Instead of trying to do everything on my own, I could accept help from others. Relying on others was out of my comfort zone—all the more reason to go. The cruise was taking place over a weekend, and really what was my choice: stay at home alone with the boys and be miserable, or have company? When I left the salon, she said it again: "You have to come, Vinnie. We'll all be there to help you." I was nervous about it, but on the drive home, I decided we should go.

Normally, if Joey and I were going on a trip, we would plan it well in advance and then enjoy every second of the wait until it came round. If we were having a rough day taking care of the boys, we would cheer ourselves up with the thought of the upcoming trip. We enjoyed the waiting as much as we did the actual trip. This trip was different, though. It felt weird not having him there to share it. And as the day approached, I had second thoughts. Part of me felt relieved that I would have adult company, but another part of me was nervous. The boys were young. It took the two of us working together to pull off a vacation, and here I was going off on a cruise alone with both boys. I understood that my friend and the other firefighters' families had good intentions in wanting to help me, but I knew it would be a lot of work. Taking care of toddler boys requires energy! What if, no matter how well-intentioned they were, when they realized the work and time required, they couldn't follow through? I went back and forth in my mind, but in the end I decided to go because the ship provided childcare. At least I'd have back-up.

The next morning I explained to the boys they would be going on a big boat. I told them they could go in a pool and that there was a place for them to play and that our friends would be there. They seemed excited. At their young ages their emotions always reflected mine. I was their barometer. If I was excited, they were excited. If I was sad, they were sad, so I tried to feel happy about the trip. I couldn't trick my heart—I wanted Joey to be with us—but I put on a brave face for the boys.

It was November 9, 2001, almost two months after we'd lost Joey. My neighbor offered to take care of Chelsea and Durante while we were gone. He drove us to the ship and said he'd pick us up on Monday morning. When we arrived at the pier, I put the boys in their double stroller and headed toward the security check-in. As I pushed them up a ramp, I thought about how much my life had changed in just two months. Usually if I was in Manhattan, I was at work, but now here I was leaving on a cruise from a dock in the city. Strange. As I leaned into the stroller, it got heavier and heavier. I wished that Joey was there to push his share of it. For a moment I thought about turning around, but something made me continue on. We went through security, and when I got to the ship's entrance, I was given a warm greeting along with keys to our cabin. The crew took our bags and the boys ventured toward our room. To my relief it was good-sized. We had a balcony and, had it not been cold, we would have used it. The bed was large enough for the three of us, and there was a bunk above that the boys immediately gravitated toward.

I changed both Vincent and Sal and set out on foot with them— hoping to run into someone we knew. I had never been on a ship before, and the boys and I wanted to explore. There were people everywhere, but I did not see a familiar face. After a couple of hours and still not seeing a single face I knew, I began feeling a bit nervous, but continued to walk with the boys hoping we would run into someone. After another hour, I started to feel fragile. I hid it from the boys. Still, I wondered if we would ever find anyone we knew. Were they looking for us?

Navigating the ship with the boys was a challenge, but we found amazing places: a huge atrium, an ice rink, a theatre, a large shopping mall that looked like an actual village, and a big pool. It was extravagant, and I could appreciate it, but it was lost on the boys. They had more practical things on their little minds, like lunch. Luckily for us I found one of several restaurants. It was roomy and bright, and there was food everywhere that looked and smelled delicious. The host asked me, how many for lunch? When I heard myself say three, I got a pain in my stomach. I could hear the host tell his assistant, "Party of three." Three. We were no longer "even." We were "odd"—an odd party of three.

Surely we would see familiar faces in the restaurant, but no. I was glad it was buffet-style. When you have hungry toddlers, you need to feed them fast, which I did, and the boys loved it. My appetite had still not returned, so I ate as much as I could tolerate. We were surrounded by luxury, but all I could feel was the deepening reality of what it meant to be on a vacation without Joey: I would never again take a vacation with him.

After leaving the dining room, we walked around the common areas and I became increasingly nervous, as I still did not see anyone I knew. This trip was a big bad mistake and I increasingly felt like I wanted to go home. I did not have cell phone numbers for the people I knew, and I was now convinced, given the size of the ship, I would never find them. At the brink of giving up and going back to the cabin, I spied a familiar face. I was so grateful when she told me where everyone was.

⁓

I walked toward the group, but noticed right away their mood was very different than mine. They were mostly the surviving firefighters from Joey's firehouse along with their wives and girlfriends. They had all been through a lot in the past weeks, and they deserved to be on this trip. They were drinking, laughing, and having a good time. I should not have come. I was one of only two widows from our firehouse. The other one was with her sisters. Her kids were older and had stayed home. When I learned this, I felt even more out of place. My friend from the salon seemed to pick up on my discomfort. "Why don't you go look at the spa and book some treatments?" she suggested. "Remember, the ship has childcare facilities. And I'll watch the boys so you can go."

Everything on the ship was complimentary, except for the spa, but that was fine with me. I was grateful for the gift of the cruise,

127

well aware I needed pampering, and relieved I had an opening to take time for myself. With the promise of childcare for the boys in the back of my mind, before even leaving shore, I'd looked over my budget and, now reviewing the spa menu, knew I could book several sessions for the coming days—just what I needed. Even in the spa lobby I felt comfortable with its soothing music and muted lighting, and every minute I was there I could feel myself breathing more deeply.

In the two months since Joey had been killed, I had not had a weekend break from taking care of the boys. My body had become tight and twisted. My muscles ached and I was always tense. I was optimistic that the treatments would work wonders since just standing in the lobby was already having such a positive effect. Suddenly I was glad to be on the ship. I would be cared for and in turn I would have more energy to care for the boys.

When I got back to the group, I told my friend about the appointments I had booked, then said I wanted to check out the childcare. She was eager to check it out as well, so off we went together. The ship was so large, the childcare facility had to be spacious. I was excited to see all that the boys would get to do. As we stepped in, I was thrilled; the place looked great, but I was shocked to discover Sal and Vincent were not welcome because they were not potty trained, and the minimum age for childcare was two. Why had this information not been available before? Or had it? Had I missed something? Joey would have known. My heart sank and panic washed through me. What was I going to do for three days? I had to get back to the spa quickly to cancel my appointments.

My friend's kids were old enough to be admitted, and she was filling out forms when I told her I had to get back to the spa. "I have to cancel my appointments."

"No, don't," she said. "I'll watch the kids while you take your first appointment. The others will help, too."

Feeling her sincerity, I didn't cancel. I was uncomfortable, but I knew I needed to trust that I was not alone. I had to believe that I would be supported.

When the time came for my appointment, I felt sure I was imposing. I sensed my friend regretted her offer when she asked what time I would return. Whether it was paranoia or the truth, it's hard to say. The stress of that time distorted so much. Still, my experience was that I was a nuisance.

First on the agenda was an essential oil massage, specifically designed for relaxation. Boy, did I need it. Ironically, as I lay on the massage table, all I could think about was the boys and whether they were a burden on my friend or her husband. I hoped and prayed that the boys were not a problem and that they were all having a good time.

When I got back from my appointment, I thanked them from the bottom of my heart, then stayed with the other families until dinner. This was the first time I had been with the firefighters since Joey's memorial. Not everyone from Joey's firehouse was there, but those who were seemed to be there to have a good time and to relax. There was a shared sense that life was fragile. They needed to let loose and enjoy themselves. They certainly deserved to, but seeing all this made me even more uncomfortable asking them to watch Sal and Vincent. What to do? I needed to pursue those things that would help me relax, just as they needed to do the same. We were escaping different worlds. I wanted to believe they all wanted to help me, but deep inside I knew they were not there to babysit.

My next spa appointment was on Saturday afternoon and I took my friend up on her offer to help. She seemed to really understand how important the appointment was for me and so I left, grateful that she cared. My muscles had been in knots ever since I stayed up night and day praying for Joey's return, and the care I received helped me physically as well as emotionally. It was nice to have validation, even if it was from a stranger, that the physical pain I was feeling from losing Joey was not in my head. The massage therapist could feel it, and that made me feel better.

The therapist suggested that I buy some bath salts that would help me relax at home. As I had the evening before, I stocked up on what I knew was little more than placebo—what I really needed was Joey. I thanked the massage therapist and hurried to pick up the boys.

They were with a group of the women gathered for lunch. The boys had already eaten and were playing with my friend's husband and their children. All was well. I ordered lunch and sat with the women. As my food arrived, one of the women spoke up: "What's in the bag?"

"Wonderful bath salts." I smiled.

"I saw you with a bag yesterday when you came back from the spa. I bet you've spent a lot of money at the spa. Must be nice." She smiled at the other women, and I had the distinct sense this had already been discussed.

I could feel the color drain from my face. I had no response. Feeling the unease, another woman changed the subject. They talked about the plans for the evening, but I couldn't pay attention. My mind kept playing her comment: "... must be nice, must be nice, must be nice ..."

Did she understand what she had said? I was sure she had not.

Must be nice?

She had her husband. He was alive and well. They had each other. They could enjoy being on a free vacation together.

Must be nice?

Every second of every day, I missed the life that Joey and I had together, and I was now experiencing firsthand what it felt like to be on a vacation without him. As these thoughts flew through my mind, the woman's husband came over and kissed her. "Come on," he said, "you wanted to go in the hot tub." She smiled at him. "I'm ready." She got up and he put his arm around her as they walked away. It must be nice, I thought to myself as I watched them walk away together. She had her husband, and I had a bag of bath salts.

At that point I no longer felt like eating. I took the boys back to the room for a nap, but they were too excited. I let them climb up to the loft bed and play with some toys I had brought from home. I felt safe in our room. There was no one there to make comments, and I did not feel like a burden.

The afternoon wore on. The boys played, and I relaxed. As dinner approached, I showered and put on a dress. It was to be a formal dinner that evening. I dressed the boys in their nicer clothes and we left our room at the very time I usually put them to bed. They hadn't napped but they seemed okay. They could both melt down when tired, so we would just eat and leave. As we walked to the restaurant, I tried to keep my focus on the fact that we were going to be with people and not alone at home. But pushing the stroller, I felt more alone than ever. I feared that my eyes would show the truth and my loneliness would be on display for everyone to see. I remember having a feeling that something bad was going to happen. Still, I carried on.

When we got to the dining room, the boys were getting sleepy and Vincent started to ask me for his binky (pacifier). I looked for it, and it was nowhere to be found. I tried to distract him with some bread from the table. I was sitting on the end of the table, not near the other mothers. Vincent wanted to go to sleep, but he could not sleep without his binky. He always had his binky when he went to bed, and now he was tired, and he needed it. I tried desperately to find it, knowing that Vincent would soon come unglued without it. I searched and searched. Surely I had brought more than one. Joey would have packed a spare binky. If Joey were here, I would have a binky. The two of us together would never forget his binky. If Joey were here, Vincent would not be upset. Everything would be fine.

In seconds Vincent was crying. I searched even more frantically. Vincent cried harder. I looked over and over in my bag. I searched the stroller. His cries grew louder. "Where is the fucking binky?" I muttered through gritted teeth. I was trying to stay positive, trying to search, but the truth was, I was traumatized. I was starting to come unglued. I could not handle the missing binky or my crying child. As he cried I could feel it in my soul. My mind was going a mile a minute: I need Joey to help me. How could I have forgotten a back-up binky? What the hell is wrong with me? For a second during all the craziness I looked at the group sitting at the table. They were having a good time. They hardly noticed Vincent or me. It was like we were in two different universes, on two different boats.

Eventually Vincent's cries got louder and were hard to ignore. Some of the other families were noticing what was happening and asked me how they could help. I explained that I needed a pacifier. No one had one. I did not expect them to. I started to feel overwhelmed. I stifled tears as I held Vincent in my arms. I wanted so badly to be able to provide him with comfort. His screaming mirrored how I was feeling—in pain, a total inconvenience, to everyone.

I was about to leave when Tony got up and came over to me. "I'll find one for you."

"Thanks, Tony, but it will be best if we go back to our room."

"Nah, give me a few minutes. I'll get you one."

I walked around with Vincent hoping to distract him during Tony's absence. Sal was sitting with one of the firefighters and his wife, so he was okay. As I walked I must have asked a dozen families with toddlers if they had a spare binky. As each said no, and Vincent became more and more distressed, I found it harder and harder to push back my own tears. I had to get out of there. Just as the tears were about to fall, Tony walked toward me. He had a binky in his hand. I felt a wave of relief. He gave it to Vincent and Vincent immediately stopped crying. I was able to put him in his stroller. I joined Sal and ate dinner with him as Vincent fell asleep. Sal almost lasted to dessert, but was tired, too, so we left.

In the room, I felt better. I could hide. No one could see the pain on my face. As I lay in bed that night, I felt shattered. I was not ready for any of this: Being away from our home, being out in public attempting a weekend vacation. None of it felt right. It would only be right with Joey by my side. I did not like life without him. I thought about the comment at lunch and how loudly Vincent had cried at dinner. It was too painful to think about, so instead I thought about the kindness of Tony and of my friend, and I went to bed feeling grateful. Tomorrow would be a better day.

The next day was better. I spent most of it with the other families and with the boys. Most of the day flew by, and I was able to go to another spa appointment with no problem. A teenage daughter happily played with the boys. I offered to pay her as a babysitter, but she said she enjoyed being with them and that she would be bored otherwise. I left with a clear head and was able to relax knowing that I was not imposing on anyone.

By Sunday, our last day, the spa treatments had done their magic and while there had been many awkward moments, I did feel more relaxed. My last appointment, booked in the late afternoon, was timed so that I would be done in plenty of time before an evening dinner ceremony. One of the firefighters who had worked with Joey, and his girlfriend, said they would watch the boys for me. Since we'd had a good day and the boys were in such a great mood, I decided to take them up on the offer. I was relieved that it was the last appointment though. It was still not easy for me to accept help.

When I got to the spa, they were running late. My appointment was pushed back fifteen minutes. It did not seem like a big amount of time, so I waited. When it was over, I rushed out of the spa. I did not want to be late picking up the boys. When I got to where they were supposed to be, no one was there. I had no idea where to look for them. I checked my room. Not there. I ran to my friend's room. She was in and told me where they were. She also told me the firefighter and his girlfriend were pissed off. I felt so bad. I went to the couple and apologized to them. I wanted to crawl into a hole. They would be late for the ceremony and it was my fault. I took Sal and Vincent back to our room.

After we got dressed, we, too, went to the ceremony, but it was no place for toddlers, so I took the boys to a buffet that was still open. There I ran into some of the families and they invited me to go out with them. There was a casino on the ship and they were all headed there. "I'm going to put the boys to bed," and though one of the guys said his teenage daughter could watch the boys, I declined, thanking him. Back in the room I felt a sense of comfort and security. There was no other place I wanted to be. I felt confused by all that had happened, my needs colliding with those of others. I'd never had to juggle this before. With Joey, we had a system. Oh how I missed him.

We all got into our pajamas and curled up. I read Sal and Vincent a story. At the end, they were still awake, so I put on the television—the movie *Shrek*—and I found myself enjoying it just as much as they were. We all snuggled up in my bed to watch. Just then there was a knock at the door. Some of Joey's friends invited me to go to the casino. I was sure the word had gotten around about how I had returned late inconveniencing our friends. I knew these kind men understood I felt bad about it. They were the ones who showed up at the door. I was touched that they wanted me to join them and have fun. One of the guys had his daughter with him. She was ready to babysit if I wanted to go, he told me.

"Thank you so much," I said, "but I truly want to stay here." I closed the door quietly and eagerly returned to bed. I pulled the boys in on both sides of me and we tumbled together into the movie. It was the best night I'd had since Joey had died. The past days had often felt like the cruise had lived up to its name—a cruise to nowhere—but now we had arrived. We were a family, and for the first time it was okay to be just three, a party of three.

Another Plane Crash

WE WERE PROBABLY SOME OF THE FIRST PEOPLE TO LEAVE THE
ship the next morning. My neighbor was there waiting in my van
with his two sons. He took our bags and the stroller and put it all
in the back, and I buckled the boys in. As we were about to leave,
his phone rang. He was a high-ranking police officer and, from his
reaction, I knew something awful had happened. The call had come
from our local precinct, he said when he got off. A plane had just
crashed two blocks from our street. It was a commercial jet. We
stared at each other in disbelief. I thought about the people on the
plane and the people on the ground. Surely there would be a lot of
injured and dead. It was November 12, 2001, too close to 9/11.

As a police officer just called to an accident scene, he had to drive
fast. We sped the whole way back to Rockaway, speculating en route
about what might have happened. Was it another terrorist attack?
I silently said a prayer for the people who must have died as well as
their families.

When we reached the area, my neighbor parked and then leaped
from the van and ran toward the scene of the crash. I was left there
with eight little eyes looking at me for an explanation. Thick black
smoke blew around us full of a strange odor. People ran everywhere.
Some men had garden hoses in their hands. Others seemed to be

running away. The neighborhood included a large number of police officers and firefighters, and many of them had been home when the plane crashed, so there was some sense of order as they assisted the emergency responders.

Oddly, I was not scared or nervous. In the midst of this catastrophe I was calm. It was such a contrast to how I felt on the ship. I had spent three weeks of my life full of fear, worrying if Joey was dead. My nightmare had already come true. A plane crashing in our neighborhood did not frighten me. If the boys, the dogs, and I died, then at least we would all be together again. Living without Joey and raising two boys alone scared the shit out of me. Death didn't.

I drove the van as far as I could. There was a roadblock a few blocks from my home. I got all four boys out of the van and tried to go home by foot but was stopped by the police. I called a neighbor and she told me to go to a house five blocks away. Her friend said we could stay there. After waiting there for a couple of hours, I felt like I had to go home. I thought about walking along the beach. We could get to my street from the beach. I walked with the four boys, ages one through four. Slowly we made our way along the sand. When we got close to our block I could see black smoke billowing everywhere. When we got to my house and I opened the door, it smelled like smoke. The smoke from the crash was blowing in the windows; there was no way to avoid it. The best that I could do was to keep them open and hope for the smoke to clear. I was able to get a neighbor to watch the boys while I ran to get Chelsea and Durante from the neighbor's backyard. They had spent the entire morning outside and must have been shaken by the explosion. Thankfully they seemed fine, and I was relieved to bring them home where I knew they would be able to rest.

As soon as we were home and I spoke to my neighbors, I realized how lucky we were to have been on that ship. The explosion had been so loud and its vibration so powerful that it had knocked my next door neighbor Denise right off her couch. I was relieved that the boys were spared that experience. The time that the plane had crashed was the very time we would have been at our regular appointments at the chiropractor's office. Had we been there, we likely would have witnessed the whole thing. It felt like someone was looking out for us. It had to be Joey.

Our neighborhood was buzzing after the crash, and my phone was ringing constantly. Every television network was calling me for an interview. My phone number was unlisted. I'm not sure how they got it. It was a big news story, a plane crash two months after 9/11, killing all on board and a few people on the ground in a neighborhood that had lost so many at the World Trade Center. They wanted to interview anyone in the neighborhood who had lost a family member on 9/11. There were so many families in the area whose loved ones had died that I had a sense, after I declined, they were already dialing the next person. It seemed like we had all felt the same way. Not one of us was interested in being on camera and being exploited. I got calls from all the major networks as well as television shows, including *Entertainment Tonight* and *A Current Affair*. My phone never stopped ringing.

By the next morning the church parking lot was full of vans with satellite dishes from different networks and television shows. The media circus had come to town. There were still memorials going on for the victims of 9/11. The streets around the crash were closed, and the plane had caused a huge crater where some houses used to be. Walking around the neighborhood and avoiding camera crews took some strategy, as they were everywhere.

A week after the plane crash I was contacted by a producer for CBS Evening News. He wanted my opinion regarding undocumented workers who were killed on 9/11. I was hesitant to give an interview because of the crash, but I did feel that the families of undocumented workers should get compensation. I agreed to speak only with the understanding that the plane crash was not mentioned. The producer kept his word and we didn't talk of it.

It took a good month for all of the news vans and their satellite dishes to leave the area and for our neighborhood to be quiet again. After the crash, the planes were supposed to stop flying over our houses, and for a short period they did, helping everyone to relax. But then one day they were flying again, and life was back to normal, at least for some people.

Healing

I REMEMBER SOMEWHERE IN THAT WASH OF MONTHS AFTER 9/11 going to the doctor for a routine checkup. "Are you sleeping?" he asked. "If not, I can give you some sleeping pills. Are you anxious? I can give you anti-anxiety medicine. Are you depressed? I can give you antidepressants."

I appreciated that he wanted to help, but I did not want to take drugs. I had spoken to another widow who was taking an antidepressant and she told me how weird she felt being on the drug. She knew she was sad that her husband had died, but being on the antidepressant she did not feel it. She didn't want to feel it. I understood why she did not want to feel it. After losing my father, I had pushed down any feelings of sadness, only to have them show up a year later. For me, trying not to feel sad about Joey's death would be like playing a game of Whack-A-Mole: I could push it down, but it would only pop up again

I had to feel the pain and sadness. There was no way around it. It was part of the natural order of things. I knew this the day I sat at Joey's memorial and listened to the words being read that I knew so well: "To everything there is a season, and a time to every purpose under heaven . . . A time to laugh and a time to weep, a time to dance and a time to mourn." It was my time to mourn, like it or not. I made my decision not to fight it. I would allow myself to feel it. In turn I hoped to heal naturally.

Still, I knew that as I faced my emotions, I would need a way to stay balanced. The only natural way I knew to do this was through exercise. I knew that if I kept my body active it would raise my mood. The natural chemicals that my body made during exercise would be crucial in my healing. I had to get my heart beating faster and the blood and oxygen flowing. I started to run and on alternate days roller blade. With the boys in daycare, I was also free to take the dogs for long walks, and I also walked alone on the beach. The combination of the waves crashing and my fast pace forced my feelings to the surface. I cried and prayed on one way down the beach, and on the way back I felt comforted by a voice of wisdom. I did feel better, but all the exercise in the world could not take away the pain I felt in still desiring Joey. I was unprepared for the physical longing. No one and nothing had prepared me for this aspect of grieving. It seemed taboo to be grieving and thinking of sex, but I was. I was thirty-four years old, still breast-feeding a baby, and at my sexual peak. My body wanted and seemed to need sex. This was a pain that I could not heal. I did not want to have sex to have sex. I wanted to have sex with Joey. I wanted to feel him and the pleasure that we always shared. I did not realize how much of a role sex had played in my life with him. It's not like I took it for granted. It was just always there and part of our relationship. I missed him so much and wanted him so much physically that I would ache for him and ultimately, when talking with friends, our sex life would always come up. It would be safe to say that by November, most of my friends knew Joey's exact dimensions.

At night I woke often from a recurring dream: Joey and I were in bed and just as we were about to have sex, something happened to prevent it. He either left or told me he couldn't do it or suddenly got up to retrieve something and didn't come back. The dream was always vivid and felt very real. I'd wake up sad, confused, and empty.

Even when I was not dreaming about him, the nights were when I thought about Joey the most. It hurt when I realized he was no longer next to me. I would remember every detail of his body and how it felt when we made love. All I wanted was to feel him again and be in his strong arms. I ached for his touch, his kiss, and the passionate nights we'd had. It was torture. Sometimes I would laugh at the thought of his antics, only to cry at the thought that there would be no more. I thought about our life after Vincent was born. We both agreed that we did not want any more children so Joey had a vasectomy. Before the vasectomy we used to have sex around three times a week, but after it he wanted sex almost every night. I asked him, if I had suddenly become more attractive. He said he'd always been afraid of getting me pregnant. He made me laugh, but it was true. We were both afraid of having more kids. When we knew it was safe, we were like rabbits. Even if we both went to bed exhausted, in the middle of the night he would roll over while I was sleeping and start to kiss me, and then before I knew it, we were making love. I always wanted him, even if I had been enjoying a deep sleep. After Sal was born we went through an adjustment period where we were so exhausted from being up all the time that I doubted we'd ever have sex again. Once we got the hang of being parents, though, we were back to normal. After that, the boys never got in the way of our desire. We would wait until they were asleep and often went from reading *Winnie the Pooh* in their bed, to making love in ours.

There were many times that Joey's passion for me arose from my cooking. For Joey, cooking was the ultimate act of love, and it turned him on. My favorite memory was one Sunday when I was cooking him meatballs and sauce. He came up behind me while I was stirring the sauce and started kissing my neck, and before I knew it, he had picked me up and carried me into the bedroom— but not before he'd turned the flame down. God forbid we ruin the sauce! I remember as he carried me to the bedroom I still had the wooden spoon in my hand and my apron on.

There were even times during the day when the kids were around that he would say, "Want to do it?" We'd lock the bathroom door, only to hear the boys knocking. In between gasps of pleasure and laughing at our predicament, we'd say together: "Be right out." I laughed to myself at thoughts of all the places we'd had sex in our house. My laughter would turn to tears, then, when I remembered Joey's sense of humor and how I would never have it again, or his touch.

༄

After Thanksgiving I started to think about Christmas. What would it be like without Joey? Our last Christmas had been our first as a family of four. I could still see Joey hanging Vincent's ornament on the tree. It said, Baby's First Christmas. He had Sal in one arm and Vincent in the other as he helped them trim our tree. We were so excited that year; the boys opened their presents with the dogs at our side. Our family was complete. I could never have imagined that it would be Joey's last Christmas.

Our first Christmas without him would be painful, and I worried about how Sal and Vincent would feel. I wanted to create some sense of happiness for them. The place that came to mind was Disney World. It is called the happiest place on earth, and I was counting on that.

I didn't want to be there on Christmas Day or during the week that the schools were closed, so I chose the second week in December. I invited my mother and brother to come and they agreed to stay a couple of days.

About a week before the trip, I was on the phone with one of the widows from Joey's firehouse. We were talking about how we were coping and I shared with her how numb I had become. She said that she had gotten into the routine of getting up, getting her kids to school, and then crying for an hour or so. After that she'd try to get on with her day.

When I hung up the phone, I realized that I was no longer able to cry. Just at that moment, Joan phoned. I told her I was feeling numb and wishing there was something I could do about it. Joan had just run into a homeopath in our neighborhood who she thought might be able to help. The fact that homeopathy was a natural medicine appealed to me. I preferred alternative methods of healing to conventional medicine, because with certain things they were more effective. As a nurse, I believed that western medicine had its place. I took the boys for their checkups at the pediatrician, but I also took them to the chiropractor for adjustments. I found a balance between both western and holistic medicine. Having no experience with homeopathy, I made an appointment and kept an open mind.

The homeopath's name was Dr. Nancy Ghales. She was also a chiropractor. Her office was in her home, and as soon as I walked in I knew I had gone to the right place. There was a good energy that I could feel, and I liked her immediately. In order for her to make an assessment, I had to tell her details about how I felt physically, as well as emotionally. Every detail mattered and she wanted to know about the present and the past, even my childhood. I had an open mind, but I was not sure why she needed so much information. I was there for over an hour before she was satisfied that she had enough. She said that she knew the exact remedy that could help me. She went to a cabinet that was full of different blue vials, took out a vial, and gave me three tiny pills. I took them, and then I expected her to give me the vial with instructions on when to take them and how long, but instead she put the vial back in the cabinet. I asked her if I needed more and she said no. "It will work, but it might take a day or two." I couldn't see how that was possible, but she seemed so confident about it. She knew I was leaving for Disney the next morning, so she told me to call her while I was there to let her know how I was feeling.

Being an RN, I had expected a prescription for pills, but she reassured me that with homeopathy it worked differently and in harmony with my body. I left not feeling any different, except for being a little curious. I was glad I'd had experience with holistic medicine before. It was definitely different, but I'd grown used to that, and now I was hoping the three little pills would work their magic and let me feel again.

The next morning we left for Florida. I was happy that my mother and brother were coming along. When we arrived at the Orlando airport, I couldn't help thinking of what a crazy idea it really was. I kept imagining my own rendition of a familiar commercial that usually ran after the Super Bowl:

"VinnieCarla, your husband was just killed. What are you going to do now?"

"I'm going to Disney World!"

It did seem ridiculous, but I had to try to make it special for the boys.

I chose to stay at the Polynesian Resort because I stayed there as a child and had good memories of that time, and because Joey and I had stayed there on our honeymoon. I knew it well; it was full of happiness for me. The Polynesian was all dressed up for Christmas—just what I was going for: something that would contrast sharply with how dead I felt inside. The lobby was full of organza garlands, wreaths, and a large, beautifully decorated Christmas tree, as well as hundreds of poinsettias. The boys were so excited when they saw the big Christmas tree and all the decorations. I had never been to Disney World at Christmastime and the décor was impressive. I only wished that Joey could be there with us. We checked into our room, which had a direct view of the lagoon and the castle. I knew the boys would be thrilled with the view when they saw the castle lit up at night.

As we explored the grounds, I reflected on my previous visits and again felt nothing. My skin, my heart, my mind were all sedated. My mother and brother had not been to Disney since our family vacation in 1979, so they were "oohing" and "ahhing." I could see it all, but felt neither happy nor sad. I was on autopilot. I knew my decision to bring the boys there was the right one because of the joy on their faces. They loved the rides, the parades, the petting zoo, playgrounds, and the pool. I wished that I could feel just some of their excitement. I thought about those three tiny pills Dr. Ghales had given me and wondered if I needed the whole bottle. Shouldn't I be feeling something by now? Perhaps my degree of pain was beyond holistic medicine.

The following day we got up as usual and I felt a bit different, like something had shifted, but I was not sure what it was, as I was still not having much emotion, sad or happy. As we left our room to go for our breakfast with Minnie and some other Disney characters,

I realized I had forgotten the camera. We were a little early so I told my mother and brother to wait with the boys. While I was walking back to the room, I could not help wishing I would see Joey running toward me with the camera. I imagined his smiling face coming closer, and I started to feel emotional. Then, before I knew it, tears burst from my eyes and I felt overwhelmed. I walked faster toward our room and started to cry almost uncontrollably. I missed Joey so much it was a physical pain in my chest. Sadness erupted, and as I cried, I almost started to laugh. "I guess the pills have done their job!"

I could feel again, and part of me was happy, even as I cried my heart out. I sobbed that it was Christmas and Joey would no longer be there with us to celebrate, that I never again would hear his teasing, or witness him playing with our sons, riding his bike, studying at our kitchen table, or that I would never again feel his kisses or make love to him, have him to confide in, or as a partner. I cried for what felt like ages, but was only ten minutes. I knew that I had to get back to the restaurant. As I stood up to fix myself, I was aware of a wave of relief that came over me. As horrible as it was, I was grateful I could feel again.

As I walked back with the camera, I was able to really see and feel the beauty of the morning. The air was fresh and clean, and the hibiscus trees were full of bright red, pink, and orange flowers. I couldn't wait to see the boys and have breakfast with them. From that moment on I was able to feel everything, and see the humor that at the "Happiest place on earth," I found myself crying almost everywhere. My memories of our last visit with the boys made me cry. I thought of how Joey took Sal on the Goofy roller coaster, and I cried. I thought about how he put Sal on his shoulders while we walked, and I cried. I thought of how he held Vincent in his arms,

147

and I cried that he wasn't with us to witness it all again. I wore sunglasses so no one could see me, particularly the boys. I didn't want to spoil one second of their magical time. My joy came from being able to feel their happiness and excitement.

Back home, my neighbor Kevin had been watching the dogs. I'd given him the keys to my house, and he went there to feed them and walk them. At the end of our holiday, he met us at the airport and drove us home. Little did I know that he had let some of the neighbors in while we were away. When we walked in the door, there was a real Christmas tree to greet us, decorated with our very own ornaments. My neighbors Lorraine and Mary had done the work, and with Christmas Day just two weeks away I was so grateful to them. That first Christmas without Joey was marked by shattering changes, but also by the blessings of friends.

New Year's Eve

MY FRIEND KAS AND HER HUSBAND WERE HAVING A NEW Year's Eve party, and she invited the boys and me. It was to be a small party with a couple of friends and their children. I wanted to keep busy and was relieved to know I would not have to spend that night alone with the children. My plan was to have dinner and leave way before midnight. As I got ready, I thought how good it would be for all of us—the boys always had a good time playing with her children and I would get to spend time with other adults.

While the men were out of the room, Kas, her friend, and I sat around her living room sharing stories and laughing until we cried. Eventually conversation led to sex and marriage. To keep the mood light, I told them a playful story about Joey and me: even when he was not in the mood, he knew when I was.

I smiled and wiped a tear as I remembered that night in August. Joey was studying to be on the Lieutenants' list again. He had taken the test a few years before and had been put on the list, but at any time they could replace the old list with a new list of names from a more recent test. Joey wanted to make sure he was on that new list, so he was taking the test again in October 2001.

Even if Joey was up late studying, we always had time for sex. He'd study in the kitchen, and I would read in the bedroom, so he'd have a quiet environment and time alone to learn his materials. He'd usually stop around ten p.m. and then want to fool around. One evening after he had been studying for hours, I went into the kitchen, sat on his lap, and started kissing his neck.

"Vin, I can't see what I am doing. Could you move your head?"

I got up coldly. "Is this better?" I stalked out of the kitchen.

"Where are you going?"

"I am going to wash up and go to bed."

"You can't lie, Vin. You want a piece of me." He knew me so well. He was right, but I denied it.

"No, I don't. I'm tired, and I am going to bed."

"Vinnie wants a piece of the Joe," he teased.

I walked into the bathroom and he followed me. "Get over yourself, I am trying to wash my face. Go back to your books."

"Sorry, I can't do that now because you are dying for the piece of the Joe."

I started to laugh.

"Now get on the bed." He picked me up and threw me on the bed. We both laughed. He knew I'd had a long day with the boys, and he made me forget that.

We had been drinking wine. Kas raised her glass. "To Joey's dick!" We all laughed.

"God, I still love that man so much."

"It's not just the dick. You want the man behind the dick." We laughed again, but she knew exactly how I felt. It was nice to be understood.

At eleven o'clock the boys were tired. I was too. Kas rode with me to help get the boys into the house. She knew carrying two boys out of the car by myself would be tricky. By the time I pulled into my driveway the boys had fallen asleep. I was grateful that Kas was there to help. I didn't have to make a decision about which one I should carry first. Kas noticed there was a minivan in front of my house. The engine was running. When I got out of my van I could hear the engine stop. Six people approached. I knew who they were. It was three guys from Joey's firehouse and their wives.

"Vinnie, we found Joey!" The way they said it I thought, "Oh God, he's been found!" My nightmare is over. I was hearing the words I had prayed for the first three weeks he was missing. My elation lasted all of two seconds.

"His body was found next to the other guys from the ladder." I realized what this meant and immediately felt the wounds reopening in my heart. It was like 9/11 all over. I had just had one of the nicest evenings that I could have had under the circumstances. It had taken me three months to get that far. Now I was catapulted back into misery—I was not prepared for what they were saying.

Kas and I carried the boys to their beds as the firefighters and their wives walked into the kitchen. Kas stayed and we took a seat as they explained their news: Joey's body, along with some of his colleagues', had been found in the buried lobby of the Marriott World Trade Center Hotel. The hotel was crushed when the Twin Towers came down. Construction workers at the site had found Joey's body. His coat helped identify him. It read Ladder 118. That afternoon the firefighters from his ladder were going through debris close by, and were called over by the workers. They carried him out of the pit. They told me that his body was intact and that he still had his mustache. One of the firefighters said Joey's arms were over his head. Hearing this I asked if his St. Florian necklace had been found. He always wore it when he worked. It was something that I hoped to give the boys one day, but they said they hadn't seen it.

They told me they also carried out Pete Vega, a colleague of Joey's, and Lt. Regan.

Kas, who had originally planned to go back home to be with her family for midnight, stayed as the firefighters and I talked about Joey. They said they had wanted to tell me in person on New Year's Eve, as sort of a gift. They assumed I would be comforted by the news that they had found him at last. But, I was not. I felt like I had been punched in the stomach. I felt like my insides were ripped out all over again, just as I was starting to feel like I was healing a little bit.

They stayed for around an hour. I didn't drink, but found a bottle of champagne for them and gave everyone a glass to toast Joey. I remember barely functioning at that point, disassociated from the action in the house, somehow having retreated into another realm. After an hour or so they all left, and I was alone with my thoughts. I knew that Joey's parents would want and need to know, but I couldn't face telling them. His mother's screaming and wailing was still fresh in my memory. I chose instead to call Joey's brother. He picked up the phone, and I quietly told him the news. He quietly accepted the news and hung up.

No one wants to think of their loved one as remains. As a nurse, I saw people die, and it became clear that in that moment the soul leaves the body. I knew that Joey had gone and his spirit was free, so the connection to his body seemed irrelevant to me. Joey had come to me in my dream. He had made his presence felt to Vincent, and I could feel him around me. I was at peace with that. But his body showing up disturbed me on new levels.

I would have to plan a funeral service. His body would just open all sorts of wounds, particularly with my mother-in-law, who in her grief-stricken state was capable of jumping onto the casket.

I'm Picking Out a Coffin for You

WHERE DO I BURY HIM? WHERE DO I GET A COFFIN? HOW DO I get a funeral home? A tombstone? What about a cemetery plot? How the hell am I going organize a funeral in my state of mind? It took everything I had to plan the memorial two months ago. I felt lost. "Happy fucking New Year."

The fire department informed me of the steps I needed to take in dealing with Joey's body and told me they would pay for the casket and cemetery plot. I needed to get a funeral home to retrieve his body from the city morgue, pick out a coffin, contact a church to do the service, and then find a cemetery. Just your everyday to-do list.

A couple of days later, one of the officers from Joey's firehouse offered to take me to a funeral home in Rockaway and then on to the cemetery, once I had decided on one. I was so grateful for his help, as I am sure I would have crashed the car if I'd had to drive. I had called the local funeral home and after speaking to the owner/director, felt comfortable going with him. He had dealt with many of the fire department families.

After I signed the necessary paperwork, the funeral director took me to an area where the caskets were. There must have been around twenty, all different. The funeral director did a wonderful job of describing each of them. Some were cedar, some one hundred percent pine wood, others mahogany, some were brown, some black, some blue or white. Then they had coffins with different finishes from metal lacquer, matte, shiny, and then there was the hardware, some pewter, some brass, some nickel-plated. Just when I thought I couldn't take anymore, there were the interior embellishments: silk, satin, and even lace. Finally, there was the eternal rest pillow. It was like being in a restaurant with too big a menu. And the whole time, accompanying the director's elaborate descriptions, all I could hear in my head was the song Steve Martin sang in the movie *The Jerk*: "I'm picking out a thermos for you, not an ordinary thermos for you . . ." It was all I could do to keep a straight face as I replaced "thermos" with "coffin" while we examined the inventory: "I'm picking out a coffin for you, not an ordinary coffin for you . . ." I actually felt Joey's presence with me making me want to giggle. Finally the funeral director showed me the casket that he had donated to all the fire department families. It was beautiful. He was a class act and a kind man, so I felt there was a good energy around it, and I thanked him. I was treated with great respect by the director, and felt confident he would take care of Joey's body. I explained to the director that I needed to find a cemetery in Brooklyn and that even though we lived in Belle Harbor, Rockaway, for six years, which is in Queens, Joey always said he was from Brooklyn. The director suggested Greenwood Cemetery in Brooklyn, which is a famous place where a lot of famous people are buried. The property is beautiful and they even have tours. I remembered that Joey had taken me there once, because it's a historical site, so it felt like the perfect place for his body to rest. The cemetery manager at Greenwood Cemetery was also very kind, and they had a specially designated site for victims of the World Trade Center. I had a choice of a few spots, and the one I chose was on a grassy hill, which overlooked the west and had a great view of the sunset. Joey and I loved sunrises and sunsets. We would always take time to walk down to the beach to appreciate them. To see that the sun would set near the site made me feel that Joey would approve. Throughout that day I felt Joey's presence with me, trying to make me laugh in the funeral home, and as I admired the beauty of Greenwood.

Later that day, I received a phone call from my mother-in-law. She wanted to know where Joey's body was. I told her that at that moment his body was still at the morgue at the medical examiner's office. What I failed to tell her was that it was actually on its way to the funeral director in Rockaway in preparation for the funeral. She told me she wanted to see his body. I knew she was very emotional, but even so, I was shocked by her request. I didn't want her to see it. I had spoken to my father-in-law and brother-in-law earlier in the week and thought they had agreed it would be a bad idea for her to see it. What flashed through my mind were the dead bodies I had dealt with at the hospital when I worked in oncology. I recalled a patient's body I had to wrap and take down to the morgue. I remembered how different a body looks when life leaves it—like an empty husk, or a cover that's left behind. It is no longer that person, with a soul and an energy. As Joey's mother spoke, I thought of how a body changes just minutes after death, and I could only imagine the state that his body was in after three months of extreme temperatures. She would not be seeing her son. She would only see what was left of his body, and I knew in my heart that Joey would never want his mother to see him like that.

I found myself changing the subject. I told her that I wanted to keep the burial and the mass very low key and private, for family and friends, but she wanted me to have a department-wide service again which would include all members of the FDNY. The members

155

of the FDNY had been to so many department memorials and now funerals, since bodies were starting to show up. How could I do that to them again? There were at least a thousand from the FDNY for Joey's memorial. They did their duty. There was no reason for them to do it twice. I understood that all the guys from Joey's firehouse would want to be present, but nothing bigger was required. I thought about what Joey would want and about what I knew to be fair in my heart, and if that caused a further chasm between his mother and me, then so be it. I had to do what was right.

The next day I spoke to the widow of the firefighter whose body was found next to Joey. We spoke about funeral plans and consoled each other. She told me that while she was paying a visit to the funeral home in her neighborhood, her husband's body had been delivered, and she had time alone with him. She told me that I might want to stay with Joey's body, too. I said I had no desire to see his body.

"No, you won't see him, just be with the body bag."

My reaction was instant. "I have no attachment to his body. I don't want to go."

"You might regret it, Vinnie, for the rest of your life."

After I hung up the phone, I thought about what she'd said. I decided to call the funeral home. I was curious to see if Joey's body was actually there. I called the funeral director, and he told me it was and I could sit with it if I wanted to. I told him I didn't want to see his body, but maybe just sit with the bag for a while. As I was talking to him, I did find it bizarre that I was talking of Joey in terms of a body bag. He told me I could come over whenever I wanted.

"I'll be over in fifteen minutes."

As I drove to the funeral home, I was nervous, not knowing how I would feel when I got there, or what would face me. I figured he would be in a black bag and that it would be in a cabinet like I had seen on TV, or in a room where they do the embalming. When I got there, the director was waiting. He walked me to one of the rooms. I held back tears as he directed me toward the door, behind which Joey lay. I was scared of what I was going to see. As I walked into the room, it was set up like all the wakes I had ever been to. His body bag was covered by an American flag and there was a place where I could kneel in front of it. The director told me what direction Joey was lying, but I could tell by the profile.

"I'll leave you alone. If you need anything, my staff will be in my office."

When I was alone with Joey's body I just stood and stared for a while. I could see the shape where his head and chest were. As I stared, I started to feel the loss of what his body had meant to me. Seeing the shape of Joey and having him present made me want to wake him up. I knelt down beside him and started to cry. I laid my head over where his chest was and I felt his loss even more as he lay there motionless. I wanted to hold him, comfort him, feel him, and I wanted him to hold me and take away my pain. I wanted him back. I wanted my life to return to what it had been. I wanted to feel the love that was now gone. I lost sense of time and found some peace in resting my head on his chest. I wished that my mother-in-law could have been in a better state of mind and she also could have sat with me. I felt very alone. I said goodbye to the body I had known and that had been the home to Joey's beautiful soul.

As I drove home, I asked Joey if he was there with me. A song immediately came on the radio, "Wherever You Will Go," by The Calling:

If I could, then I would
I'll go wherever you will go
Way up high or down low
I'll go wherever you will go

Since Joey's death, in difficult times, this song would come on the radio. I felt him in the car with me. I was not really paying attention to my driving, and I made a wrong turn onto a one-way street. As a car passed me, the man inside was cursing me out. If only he had known I had just been with my dead husband's body, maybe he would have been more compassionate.

The Funeral

I MADE A DECISION TO SPARE THE BOYS THE UPSET OF THE funeral. Sal and I had not talked about Joey since the night I told him that his daddy had died. I knew Sal was suffering. I figured that he and Vincent had been through enough. I dropped them off at daycare and shared nothing of the plans for that day.

I remember standing in that cold air of January at Joey's graveside. I was numb from both the cold and the reality of the events that had led up to this moment. The priest was about to say the final prayer as we were all gathered around his coffin. I was standing in the front row, my mother and brother and close friends to my right and Joey's family to my left and behind me. As people were still gathering, I heard Joey's aunt explaining to another family member that I must have loved him even though I was not acting like it. I was a mystery to most of his family. In their eyes I wasn't playing the role of grieving widow. This was the stage, and I was meant to perform. I knew the requirements: screaming, wailing, and black clothing, and I knew I could have impressed them if I'd made a dive for the coffin. That would have sold them on my love for Joey, but I couldn't. My mother-in-law, as I expected, was attempting to jump onto the casket and go down with him. I was glad when the day was over and I could go back to my private, sad life.

Joey's Last Minutes

A FEW DAYS AFTER THE FUNERAL, I RECEIVED A PHONE CALL from the firehouse: an elevator mechanic who had worked at the Marriott World Trade Center Hotel wanted to talk to me. He had information on Joey's last moments.

Now I could find out what had happened. I agreed to talk to him. He called and told me that he had been with Joey and the other men in Joey's ladder on 9/11. He said the Marriott was chaotic after the planes hit the Towers. A swimming pool on the twenty-second floor cracked, possibly from the vibrations that the two planes had made upon impact. The water flooded the elevator shafts and trapped fleeing guests on different floors. Wearing helmets labeled 118, the firefighters ushered many guests out of the hotel. He told me that because of the flood many elevators had become stuck with people inside. He was trying to pry open one with a crowbar but without success. Joey had knelt down next to him, used a tool to open it, and the people ran out. At one point, they opened up an elevator door to find a man in a wheelchair, and Joey had carried the man to safety. Then Joey joined the firefighters in the lobby. They were directing people away from the West Street exit, where steel girders, debris, and bodies were raining down. The firefighters made a human wall to make sure no one went out the wrong way.

The last thing the elevator mechanic heard was the Lieutenant's voice from Ladder 118 yelling, "Stay away from the window! This place may come down!" What had astonished him was that as he ran for his life, the firefighters stood firm in the same spot. Minutes later the hotel was hit by the collapse of the South Tower and then obliterated under the mass of the North Tower. He said he'd been buried by debris. He crawled out and turned around to look at where the firefighters had all been standing—and everything was gone.

I thanked him for sharing his story about my husband. It confirmed what I knew in my heart. Joey died helping people.

Valentine's Day

AFTER 9/11, MY NEXT-DOOR NEIGHBORS MIKE AND DENISE, who had been casual acquaintances, became two of my closest friends. They were newlyweds who had married and moved in during the summer of 2001. They had a great relationship and seemed to really understand my loss. Evenings in October, I would often sit outside on my porch, with my baby monitor, because I could not sleep. Mike and Denise would stay outside and talk with me. Eventually, it got colder and they would welcome me into their home. It became a routine that a few times during the week, I would put the boys to bed and then take my baby monitor to their house. It worked because our houses were so close together. If the boys woke up and called for me, I was there in a quick moment. We would talk and listen to music or watch movies from eight to around ten o'clock. I wanted to always give them time to themselves and would never stay past ten. They were wonderful company, and being with them took the sting out of Joey's loss. They were not uncomfortable with my grief or how much I talked about Joey. I never had to hide my true emotions. If Mike and Denise invited me over on nights that I could not stop crying, they said, "You know, Vinnie, we do have tissues." I would go over then and even if I cried, I would always feel better in their company. Since I was having a lot of trouble sleeping, Denise always made me a cup of chamomile tea. It helped. I fell asleep easier when I got home. They adopted me as a sister and always made me feel welcome. If I had not had their company in the evenings, I would have gone crazy from loneliness.

One of the things we had in common was a love of Mexican food, and at least once a month we'd go to a Mexican restaurant in Bay Ridge, Brooklyn, called Casa Pepe. The food was amazing, and I would even have a margarita or two. The atmosphere was light and fun and we always had a good time, often laughing until we cried.

When February rolled around, Mike and Denise invited me to go out with them on Valentine's Day. I did not think it was right to go with them; they were newlyweds, but they said they would not take no for an answer. I appreciated the kindness and compassion they showed me, but the truth was Joey and I hadn't really celebrated Valentine's Day, and even though I told them that, they still wanted me to come. In a short amount of time, they'd gotten to know me well; they knew I would not be okay home alone on a day that celebrated love. I agreed to go, and we went to the sister restaurant to Casa Pepe's, Tia Pepe, which was in Greenwich Village. The food was just as good as Casa Pepe, but there was definitely a different vibe. The restaurant was situated in the middle of the West Village among the sex shops. After dinner, Denise told Mike that she and I were going to take a little walk, while he walked to get the car. Across the street from the restaurant was a store called The Pink Pussycat. It was filled with sex toys. Having heard my tales about Joey's penis, Denise felt it would be a good idea if I bought one. I was a clueless virgin when it came to vibrators. I had been married to a man who satisfied me. Now I found myself alone at night and unskilled at the art of self-fulfillment.

Having a few margaritas gave me courage, and knowing Joey's anatomy in detail, I picked out one that was as close to him as I could find. Denise and I giggled like two little girls as I pointed out the one I wanted to the guy behind the counter. This was a most unusual Valentine's Day, I thought, as I paid for my fake dick. I was sure it would remain in the bag, but it felt fun and adventurous to have it.

Mike was outside and laughed at us when he saw me holding my pink bag. As we rode home, I felt so grateful that I had Denise and Mike as friends, and that I could have fun with them. I had the sense that Joey was there with us and that he did like them, but it wasn't enough. I was getting used to this feeling—having a good time but feeling his loss at the same time. I wondered if I would always feel this way.

When I got home and the buzz had worn off, I looked at the bag in disgust. I was grateful for Mike and Denise and our fun evening, but this was not me. I hid the bag in my closet. I wanted Joey, not a piece of plastic.

Suze Orman and the Gift of Empowerment

IN EARLY MARCH, THE MEDIA WERE STIRRING UP STORIES about the amount of money that 9/11 families were receiving, specifically stories about the 9/11 Compensation Fund and millionaire widows, and the public was eating these stories up. The FDNY families, it seemed, were particularly portrayed as rich and greedy, a framing that felt like such an attack; we were grieving families with loved ones lost forever. I told myself it wasn't really personal; it was business. Stories like that sold papers, and I took solace in the fact that people who knew me personally understood that no amount of money could make up for the loss of Joey, but I was wrong. After avoiding the spotlight that accompanied the local plane crash, I fell victim to an invasion of my privacy on a different, more hurtful scale.

It began with little things, but they added up. At the salon where I got my hair done, I discovered that after the stories appeared in the papers, I was being charged three times the amount other customers were paying for products. When my friend asked her boss why she charged me so much, she was told: "She can afford it." I no longer purchased her products after learning what she was doing, and while I was hurt by the behavior, it seemed like a minor pettiness.

Then a neighbor who knew I was planning to either finish the renovation on my house or sell it offered me less than the market value. In his eyes, I already had enough money.

When it snowed and my neighbor Mike shoveled my sidewalk, another neighbor said he should not bother since I had enough money to hire someone to do it.

A close friend, a nurse whom I had worked with at the hospital, dealt the heaviest blow. She was very compassionate toward me in the first weeks after 9/11. Her sister's husband had also been killed at the World Trade Center, so she had a good idea of what I was going through. She would often call to see how I was doing and then tell me about how her sister was coping. Unfortunately, her sister was not doing well in those early months. Relatives were taking turns caring for her and her children and yet her sister was often ungrateful toward them. Despite this, they kept taking care of them.

For five months we talked once a week and supported each other. After the newspapers ran the stories about the 9/11 Compensation Fund, I received a call from her. She was particularly upset. She complained that her sister's standard of living had gone down since her husband's death. She had lived in a large home in Larchmont, New York, and had been a stay-at-home mother of three. She'd had a housekeeper, two nannies, and club memberships. Now she was depressed that her husband was gone and she would not be able to maintain her lifestyle.

"I understand how she misses her husband—"

"I doubt you could understand how she is feeling," my friend snapped. "My sister is losing her money! She was not married to a firefighter, you know. You have more money than you did when Joey was alive. Your life is better! My sister's is worse."

I was speechless. This was my friend. I thought she was my friend. Almost out of breath from the blow, I told her I had to go. I never heard from her again.

The amount of money the stories reported was not accurate, but it hardly mattered. Once circulated, the ideas persuaded some people that any pain or loss I was feeling over Joey had been absolved by money. I think it was easier to be angry at us—at anyone—to point fingers and identify villains after 9/11 than to take in the awkward complexities of the devastation.

The media attention did more than just change the way we were viewed. It also served as an advertisement. I received many calls from different brokers who told me that they would be happy to help me invest my money. I had worked for a securities company before becoming a nurse and had seen some brokers take advantage of people. Some even bragged about it. I was starting to feel a need to protect myself from the sharks and the vultures. I did not want to be taken advantage of, but I knew that I needed to get some advice on how to handle family finances.

Knowing what all the families were dealing with, the firefighters at Joey's firehouse tried to help in any way they could. One of them had a broker who wanted to help, so it was arranged that we would meet with her. I liked the fact that the broker was a woman. I wanted to believe that there was a sisterhood out there of women helping one another.

When I arrived at the meeting, a restaurant in Brooklyn, most of the other widows and family members were already there. And when the broker introduced herself, my immediate reaction was suspicion. Something didn't feel right, and when she began speaking, my gut feeling was confirmed. Her discussion about investing seemed purposely misleading and confusing. All she knew of me was that I was a registered nurse; I hadn't divulged my securities company experience; and to test her, I asked a simple question: what is a dividend? Instead of answering in a comprehensible way, she made it seem like rocket science. Just to make sure I was not wrong, I asked some more. Again and again, she made answers far more complicated than they were.

Well, so much for the sisterhood.

As the broker ended her talk, she dealt out business cards—like cards at a poker game. I took her card and thanked her, but when I left I threw it away. I was not sure if the rest of the women or family members had the same reaction I did. The only thing I felt for sure was that we were still in need of advice, and we needed it to come from someone who had our best interest at heart. Where were we going to find that?

On the drive home, I could not get one widow out of my head. She seemed so confused. Her husband had handled their money. She had never even balanced a checkbook. The thought of this woman being taken advantage of plagued me. I did not have enough knowledge to help her or myself, but I had to do something. Since I had no idea what, I prayed about it.

Two nights later in the middle of the night unable to sleep, I turned on PBS. On the screen I saw my answer, Suze Orman. She was giving a lecture on finances. She was straightforward, clear, and easy to understand. She could give us the help we needed. She could point us in the right direction. She was the one. I just had to find a way to contact her.

The next morning, I researched as much as I could about her and found her agent's name and number. At nine o'clock I would make the call. I was a bit nervous, but took a deep breath and said a prayer. The woman that answered was an assistant to her agent. I told her I was a firefighter's 9/11 widow and was hoping that Suze Orman could help me and other firefighter families with their finances. Within minutes of hanging up with the agent's assistant, the agent herself called me. She spoke in a heavy New York accent. Even though she was kind and compassionate, I could tell that she was a tough New Yorker. She had a no-bullshit way about her when she spoke. It was clear to me that she wanted to help. "It might take a few days, but I will talk to her, and I promise you that I will get back to you."

It did not take days. Within an hour, the agent called me back. Suze Orman had agreed to give a lecture for free. Ms. Orman even contacted me personally to tell me that she would be happy to help. I worked out the details with her agent. In about a month she would speak. I was still in a fog, so having never put a seminar together had me scrambling.

Trying to help the other families turned out to be harder than I would ever have thought. First, I had to contact the family assistance unit of the FDNY. There I discovered, understandably, that they could not give me a list of family members' addresses, but they did agree to let me write a letter they would mail to the families. After getting it composed, I made multiple copies, took them to their office and stuffed envelopes. I didn't mind taking the time to do it, because I felt like I was doing something worthwhile. After six months of feeling like a victim, a part of me felt empowered. I also extended the invitation to family members of the Port Authority Police Department. I wished I could have invited the thousands of families of 9/11, but I was overwhelmed dealing with hundreds. It was challenging at times to be there for the boys and to organize the event, but I knew it was energy well spent.

Another challenge was finding a venue. I wanted it to be somewhere that was convenient for the families and Ms. Orman. Manhattan was the ideal choice because of its accessibility to public transportation, but finding a place required more than one person. Luckily, Nancy Carbone, founder of Friends of Firefighters, was happy to help me find a hotel in midtown Manhattan. It cost a few thousand dollars so I had to charge a small fee to the family members to cover the cost. About a quarter of the families that I invited showed up. Their combined fees did not cover the total cost, as it turned out, but I was not upset about that. I paid the balance myself. I felt strongly this was an event that could help.

When the day for Ms. Orman's lecture arrived, I had to get there early to organize things. In addition to speaking, she also donated copies of her latest book. I unpacked the books and arranged them on a table where I would hand them out. She kept the whole thing quiet from the media. I admired that she did not look for recognition. When the families started to arrive, I realized that I would have to give an introduction for Suze Orman. I have no trouble talking to people one-on-one. Public speaking is another story. When it was time to begin, I summoned up all my courage and walked to the front of the room. Miraculously, I managed to quickly say who I was and to introduce Suze Orman.

Ms. Orman got up in front of the room and after speaking compassionately about our deceased family members, began to demystify financial terminology. She explained things in such a clear and comprehensible manner that I think even Sal and Vincent could have understood. One the most important things I learned that day was the difference between a money manager and a broker. Basically, managers made money if you made money and brokers made a commission every time they bought and sold stocks, bonds, and mutual funds. It was valuable information for all of us. She also spoke about paying off debts and why that was important. At the end, she took time to answer questions and clarify anything that seemed confusing. I was relieved that the very widow who I could not get out of mind had shown up that day.

There was a lot of pain in the room as widows and family members struggled to understand the world of finance that had been foisted upon them. No one wanted to be in the position they were in. Just six months earlier we had all been going about our lives. No one's loved one had been battling a terminal illness; they were, for the most part, healthy, thriving men. Then suddenly we were dealing with the incomprehensibility of the attack, and just as suddenly, we were dealing with the unknown. Were our loved ones dead or alive?

Many of us had gone on to memorials with no bodies. Then some of us had received bodies, or body parts, picked out coffins and burial plots, and planned cremations or funerals. It was as if we were living in a very bad dream none of us could wake up from. Daily we greeted our pain and struggled to chart a way forward, but everywhere we went there were reminders of that day. If we put on the television, within minutes we heard "9/11" spoken. The image of the buildings collapsing played over and over, and the footage of the planes hitting the buildings appeared on the news almost every night.

And then, just as it seemed money was being distributed and the relief it could offer was within reach, the funds became just one more element in a contentious, continually changing, and unrecognizable landscape that had to be negotiated by grieving and overwhelmed 9/11 family members. To many viewing us from the outside, it may have looked as if money would take care of it, make it all easy, but the reality was that each day was a new pocket of fresh pain. Everyone in that room was hurting, and that had not changed just because of public opinion.

One widow was still holding onto checks because she could not cash them. She had so much guilt related to the money. By banking it, she felt she would be saying she was okay with her husband's death. Her conflict spoke for all of us. Contrary to what others now believed, money did not change the situation: our loved ones would never be coming home, they had died in a shocking event, and closure on their deaths was open-ended since recovery efforts at the site prolonged the process a regular funeral and burial would have provided. Yes, there was comfort in knowing that on top of all of this, we probably would not have to struggle financially, but the center of our lives had been lost and nothing would ever assuage that.

As Suze Orman closed her talk, I wondered if she had expected the atmosphere that she experienced in the room that day. It was a far cry from how the media had portrayed the situation, but whatever she expected, she dealt with it in a kind and compassionate way. One thing for sure was that she had helped me. I now had some direction on how to handle things financially, and for the first time in six months, I did not feel like a victim. Even though I was heartbroken and knew I had a long road ahead, it was Ms. Orman's gift of empowerment that made me feel that Sal, Vincent, and I someday would be all right.

Finding My Way

SEVERAL WEEKS AFTER SUZE ORMAN'S LECTURE, I WAS AT MY friend Victoria's house. The boys loved to play at her house with her daughters, Ashley and Amanda. Ashley was nine and Amanda at four was six months older than Sal. Victoria was in the midst of planning her spring break vacation. Every April, her family spent a week at their timeshare in West Palm Beach, Florida. She was happily making her plans when she got this funny look on her face. "You know, Vin, you and the boys should come."

"Thanks, but I don't think I'm up for it." I remembered my last vacation with the boys and didn't have the energy for a repeat of that experience.

"You have to come, Vin. I'll be there, and so will Cynthia. Come on, Vin, her daughters will watch the boys. They have childcare, too, so you can have a break. It will be fun."

Before I could sort out my feelings and give her a firm reason for not going, she was on the phone making reservations for me. Victoria was like a sister, and we did have a lot of fun together, so I thought I would try.

Our plane arrived in Florida in the afternoon; Victoria and her family had arrived that morning. Her husband met me at the car rental area of the airport. I followed him from the airport to their hotel. When we got there, Victoria hopped into my car and showed me the way to my hotel, which was only five minutes away. It seemed effortless. The weather was beautiful. It was sunny and warm.

After I had checked in, the boys and I changed into our bathing suits and headed back to her hotel to have lunch and swim in the pool. It was a nice hotel, and the boys ran right to her daughters and they all went for a swim while I got lunch. Victoria watched the boys while I ordered their food. It was nice to be there with her. After the boys had their lunch, I sat with Victoria and her friend Cynthia and kept an eye on the boys. They were playing in the baby pool.

I thought of Joey. I couldn't help missing him, and Cynthia kept asking about him and our marriage. Victoria had told her how nice Joey was and what a great dad and husband he had been. She wanted to hear all about him. Her own marriage didn't seem happy and it seemed to do her good to hear about a man like Joey. Of course, going on about him stirred it all up for me—not that it was ever gone. Thoughts of Joey gave me comfort and made me feel close to him. I felt fortunate I'd had such a wonderful partner and father to my children. I realized that not everyone who was married was as happy as we had been. Even with my loss, I felt grateful that Joey and I had had something unique.

For the rest of the afternoon we stayed by the pool. Victoria, and Cynthia and her husband all had cocktails. I swam in the pool with the boys. I wished Joey could be here with them playing in the water. I tried not to think about him, but there were a lot of fathers and small children around. Inside, my heart was breaking.

I was used to feelings of loss and heartbreak. It was my baseline, but there was something else that was not quite right. What was it? The hotel was beautiful. The weather was heavenly . . . but then I saw it. As I watched the fathers swimming and playing with their kids, I realized that I was the only woman in the pool. The other women were on the chaise lounges with cocktails, wearing makeup, jewelry, and sarongs with bathing suits that had not touched water.

That evening we had dinner at eight o'clock, the time I normally put the boys to bed. It had been a long day. They were over tired. Vincent wiggled out of his safety belt and fell off his high chair onto his head. I thought that his head would split open or that he'd broken his neck. Miraculously, he fell in a way that protected him, but it did not matter. Seeing him fall had scared me to my core. When I picked him up, he was, screaming so loudly that it made me start to cry. I was just as tired as he was and I wanted to leave. Instead I went to the bathroom to soothe him. I got him to stop crying. I made sure he was okay and then I splashed water on my face and went back to the table. Victoria and her husband were very supportive. They helped Sal with his dinner, and Victoria held Vincent on her lap so I could eat. They wanted us to have a good time. I knew that they felt bad about Vincent's fall and the fact that we were off schedule. I did not expect them to change their habits for us. It was nice that they had invited us, and I was grateful, but it was still hard for me. I missed Joey so much and couldn't seem to get my footing in the world. Who was I without him? I hardly knew how to navigate the sea of choices. We finished dinner, and I focused on the fact that we were with friends. Then I excused myself, took the boys back to our hotel, and hoped that tomorrow would be better.

Unfortunately, it wasn't. My mother called. My grandmother had died. I told my mother I would return immediately.

"VinnieCarla," my mother said, "you have had enough death to deal with. Stay there and have a good time. Grandma would want that. You were always good to her, and she knew it. Have fun with

175

your boys." I knew my mother was right, so I stayed even though I felt out of place. I was reaching toward something. I just didn't know what it was.

Every day unfolded like the one before. The boys and I would go to Victoria's hotel. We would spend the day by the pool. Cynthia would ask me about Joey, and then I'd swim with the boys. At four o'clock, I would leave their hotel, go to mine, bathe the boys, get ready for dinner, and then head back to their hotel where we planned to meet for dinner. By the time we arrived at the restaurant, Sal and Vincent would be over tired and would crawl on the table to get to the sugar packets or the salt and pepper. I'd end up walking with them in the lobby until the food was served. Things just weren't working. But what did I want?

The next night, as the boys and I waited in the lobby, something flipped inside of me, like an activation switch. I knew I didn't want this type of vacation. I begged off for the evening and took the boys back to our hotel. In our room I scoured a magazine for descriptions of the local restaurants. I wanted to find a place that was kid friendly. As I searched, the boys happily jumped on the bed. They were having a great time, and I wished we could just stay there. When I saw the room service menu, I realized that we could. It had food the boys would enjoy. I ordered and played with the boys while we waited. It was so effortless. The food was delicious, and the boys and I were having fun together. I felt so empowered and independent.

It was at that moment that I came up with my idea. We were in Florida and I needed to be in a kid-friendly place. I quickly called Disney World. They had rooms available at the Polynesian Resort. I booked a room starting the next day for the remainder of our time in Florida. I called the airline and switched the flight. Then I called the car rental company and asked if I could drop off the car in

Orlando. My last call was to the front desk. I told them I would be checking out in the morning. I was free! And I felt so independent. I could get out of there. I did not have to stay in a situation that was not good for us. I had options. I could steer our ship in a different direction, and it felt great.

The next morning when I pulled out of the hotel parking lot and made a right instead of making the left to Victoria's hotel, I felt a sense of euphoria. As I was finding my way to the highway, my cell phone rang. It was Victoria letting me know where I could find them.

"Victoria, thank you so much for everything. It's just not working for us, so I'm leaving. I appreciate all that you've done for me."

"You're leaving? Where are you going?" She sounded distressed.

"I'm on my way to Disney World."

"Are you crazy? You're alone with the boys. Do you even know how to get there?"

"Not really, but I'm heading north, and I have directions. We'll be fine." I felt giddy with my new-found power. "I love you, Victoria. Thank you for everything." "Okay, Vin. I understand." There was no anger or animosity in her voice. She was a true friend. "Be careful. See you when we get back."

I felt such a sense of freedom, and for the first time in a long time, I felt happy. I told the boys that we were on our way to see Mickey Mouse, and they cheered and rocked in their cars seats.

On the road, I called my mother and asked her if she or my brother would like to meet me in Orlando. I knew my mother would not come—she hated to leave her house—but I thought my brother might. My mom told me that he had just taken off work to attend my grandmother's funeral and that he had no more vacation days left. I knew she could sense I was a bit nervous about going it alone. She said something that made all the difference to me: "You will be fine. Don't doubt yourself, VinnieCarla. You have always had the ability to do anything you put your mind to. You don't need anyone's help. If it were anyone else, I would be worried, but you will be fine."

She was right. I was grateful for the moments when her mind was balanced. It was then that her wisdom would shine through. She empowered me. I could feel her support and her belief in me. I knew that even though I was nervous, I was going down the right road, literally. "I love you, Mom. I'll call you when I get there."

As I drove, I felt Joey's spirit by my side. I said a prayer. I was grateful I'd had what it took to get up and go.

I had no problem finding my way. We didn't even hit traffic. I felt so good. The boys were happy. I had music on with the windows wide open, and the sun was shining. As we moved up the freeway toward Orlando, two songs came on back-to-back: "Landslide," and "Wherever You Will Go," my anthems. I took it as a sign. I was going in the right direction. In a way, I felt like I was going home.

That afternoon when I pulled up to the Polynesian Resort, I felt as if we had arrived in paradise. The hibiscus were in bloom and the palm trees were swaying in the warm breeze. By coincidence I was in the same building that Joey and I had stayed in on our honeymoon. Another good sign.

That day we played on the beach and made sandcastles. For the first time in a long time, I forgot the clock while enjoying the company of the boys. I realized I was finally where I was supposed to be and was with the two most important people in my life. I was so grateful I felt that way again. They did not feel like a burden.

That evening we ate dinner at Chef Mickey's. I did not have to worry about the kids disturbing anyone. It was a buffet. The kids could eat right away. Mickey, Minnie, Pluto, Donald, and Goofy all stopped by the table for a visit while we ate. We were in heaven.

After dinner we went back to our hotel. We could see the castle from our balcony. At night after the boys went to bed, I felt a sense of comfort and peace. I missed Joey, but I did not feel alone.

During our time there, whenever I thought I was alone, there always seemed to be someone in my path who helped me. When the boys and I were on the bus coming back from the Animal Kingdom Park and Vincent was asleep in my arms, a stranger carried my double stroller off the bus and helped me put the boys in it. Wherever I went someone helped me when I needed an extra hand. I never felt like I was alone once, and I realized that I never really would be. Help was all around me, and I finally could see it.

A Natural Woman

ROCKAWAY WAS HOME TO MANY POLICE AND FIREFIGHTERS.
A large number of the firefighters killed on 9/11 had lived in
Rockaway. In Belle Harbor, where I lived, there were at least six
firefighters I knew of on our street, which ran from the bay to the
beach. Some streets had more. It was safe to say that firefighters and
police officers lived on every block. So when word spread in our
community that firefighters were leaving their wives for FDNY 9/11
widows, it rattled up and down the streets shocking believers and
nonbelievers. Unfortunately, there were people who believed if one
widow could go off with a married man then we all could.

I never expected that anyone who knew me could ever think
that I could do such a thing. I knew that my character and actions
spoke for themselves. My values and morals were evident to anyone
who knew me, so surely I would be seen as an individual, as the
person I had always been. I was wrong.

One afternoon in May, a neighbor and I were in front of my
house watching our kids. "Your blouse is so pretty," she said.

"Thanks." I gave Vincent a push on his truck.

"Why are you wearing it?"

"What?"

"We're out here with the kids, and you're so dressed up." I was wearing a blouse with jeans and sneakers. "Aren't you afraid of what people are going to think?"

I bent down to help Sal fix a wheel on his toy car and looked up at her quizzically.

"I'm just saying that, if I were you, I would watch what I was wearing."

"What I'm wearing?" I looked down at my outfit.

"You know how people are. They may think you want to look good for the men on the block."

I could feel my spine stiffen. "What are you saying?"

"Vinnie, your hair is always done, and you look thin. I'm not saying there's anything wrong with it, but you know how people can be." She rolled her eyes.

I stood before her dumbfounded, unable to mouth even the simplest of words. She filled the gap and went on to tell me the reason one of my neighbors no longer walked my dogs: his mother-in-law had told her daughter not to allow him to be around me.

This was crazy making and I snapped. I was thinking and talking all at once. I spoke—no, ranted!—so quickly I didn't give her a chance to respond. "The only man I want is my own. My blouse! This blouse makes me feel like I'm still a woman. I don't feel much like a woman these days taking care of two toddlers, two dogs, two cats and—oh yeah! because the last time I had sex, and really felt female was on September tenth!

"My blouse? I don't look like I used to? Yeah, you're right, and I don't feel like I used to either. I'm thinner because I didn't eat while Joey was missing—for weeks! I still don't have an appetite, and I'm glad, too, because if I had one, I'd be a fat widow, and that's the last thing I want to be.

"My hair? Yes I've been getting it blown out. I'm sorry if I haven't given up and started wearing sweat pants!"

I wanted to say more but couldn't. My head was still spinning out thoughts, like how Joey's death had not changed my values or who I was, but I seemed to have lost my voice.

She apologized, but she didn't really understand.

I wanted to scream—make her hear the truth of my life which had nothing to do with wanting someone's husband. My truth was how hard it was to get up every day. How painful it was that I could never talk to the person who mattered so much to me. How impossible it felt to go through the day without sharing stories about the boys or a conversation about what was for dinner at breakfast. Or how sad I felt that Joey did not get to see me with my hair done, wearing this blouse. I would feel sexy in front of him now, thinner, but I was not going to have sex with him ever again.

Sometimes I wished people knew just how fragile I was. I was hanging on by a thread. How could I live a new life that I didn't want or plan? One day I'd think I saw a path. The next I didn't know how to live without Joey. I had always been independent, but now I was alone, and that was different. The things Joey had done for me, I had to do for myself. It was not that hard to fix certain things around the house. I knew how to use tools to repair minor things, but taking care of myself in other areas was not that simple.

One night I did try to take certain matters into my own hands, literally. I went to my closet and took out the vibrator. It was the first time it had been out of the box. It felt so weird to even hold it. Anatomically it was the same size as Joey. I took the flesh-colored plastic thing in my hand and switched it on. It made a buzzing sound, which was unnerving. Clumsily I inserted it and waited to feel something. The only thing I felt was ridiculous. It didn't do anything except make me feel pathetic. I tried to relax, but instead I analyzed why it was not working for me. Was it because I was Catholic? No, I enjoyed my physical relationship with Joey. I had no hang-ups in our bedroom and enjoyed every sexual thing we did together. Maybe this vibrator was the wrong model for me. No! I wanted the real one, the one with the pulse of the man I loved attached to it. It wasn't about an orgasm. It was about the love we shared, and I could not get that from a piece of plastic. This thing would never reach far enough inside of me the way Joey did. Only Joey could touch my soul. I hated this stupid thing. I tossed it out of my bed and started to cry. I wanted to throw it back in the closet, but being a nurse I cleaned it first. God, I'm ridiculous, I thought as I cried. Then I put the thing in its box and hid it far in the back of the closet where the boys would never find it. I laughed through my tears, imagining all the questions they would have. It would stay hidden and stay in that box. But I was not really hiding it from the boys; I was hiding it from myself. Seeing it was a reminder that Joey was really gone. I quickly shut my closet door.

What could I do to really feel better?

I walked to Joey's closet, opened it, and stuck my face into his clothes, just to smell him again. I wrapped myself in his shirts and wished I could bury my face in his chest, hug him, and have him back. I felt comfort in the scent of his clothes. As I did it, I wondered if I would become a crazy person—a crazy lady who just stayed in her dead husband's closet. Completely deranged, I could carry on with my marriage, with my dead husband's clothes—

in the memory of the man I loved and who made me feel like a natural woman.

The Documentary

I KNEW THAT MY FIRST SUMMER WITHOUT JOEY WOULD be hard. I tried to keep myself as active as I could to balance out the feelings of sadness. During the week, when the boys were at daycare, I jogged with the dogs at Fort Tilden, where it was quiet and desolate. On the weekend mornings I took the boys with me in their double jogger and roller bladed down my jogging paths, but even though I kept as active as I could, it was still hard to face the summer without him. My mind could not help remembering all the good times we'd shared.

In the summer, Rockaway came alive, and Joey and I took advantage of it all. Some days we were filled with bike riding, swimming, boogie boarding, and volleyball. Others we took slow. Living in Rockaway was like living in a resort. The beach was just steps from the house. Some days we would get to the beach in the afternoon and spend the whole day there, playing in the waves and the sand, and relaxing in the sun. We would have pizza delivered to the beach wall and watch as the sky turned amazing colors and the sun set. It was a magical time of year, and I'd thought we would have many summers there together as a family. Now I would do the best I could without him.

One June morning, I drove the boys to the chiropractor. When I pulled into a parking spot in front of a restaurant, I noticed the owner talking to a man. After I parked the car and walked around to get the boys out of their car seats, I had a strange feeling that now they were talking about me. I brushed it off as paranoia and realized that Vincent, who had a cold, had fallen asleep. I was deciding how best to pick him up without waking him, when I heard a man's voice. "Do you need a hand?" It was the man who had been talking to the owner of the restaurant. "No, I'm fine. Thanks." I was a bit suspicious of him. I had never seen him before and he certainly did not look like he lived in the area. His clothes looked too trendy and his hair was a bit long. He introduced himself as Jack and told me he was in the area making a documentary about Rockaway. Why had he come over to me? I kept to my business. As I lifted Vincent out of the car, Jack said the documentary was about 9/11. Now it made sense. He was only talking to me because the owner of the restaurant must have told him I was a 9/11 widow. I wanted nothing to do with him, even though he did seem nice. I was polite, but kept moving. He tagged along and asked if I had grown up in Rockaway. I told him I hadn't. He said that he hadn't thought so—that I had a unique look. He said it in a flattering way, and I was surprised because he seemed to be flirting. It had been a long time since a man had noticed me, let alone flirted, as I had the scarlet lettered "FDNY widow" on my forehead. I unbuckled Sal with one hand and he got out of his seat. Then this persistent filmmaker asked about my nationality. When I answered, he said I looked like an actress. I was enjoying the attention, even though I knew he was only talking to me because of my connection to 9/11, and that his compliments were inevitably calculated. I took Vincent in my arms and Sal by the hand and walked away from him.

"Do you know any 9/11 widows that I could talk to?"

I laughed. He had to know about me, but I played along. "Yes." As I reached the office door, and had some distance on him, I said, "You were just talking to one."

"Can I talk to you?"

"The boys have colds. I have to go."

We all got adjusted, and when we walked out of the office, he was still there! I was a bit amused by his action. We had been inside for about fifteen minutes and yet he waited. He walked up to me and started to talk as I made my way to my van. He told me about his documentary. I listened, but did not give him my full attention. I put the boys into their car seats. "Can I talk to you? I would like to ask you questions about your husband."

I had a distaste for the media after all the negative stories. I figured he was out to exploit 9/11. Trying not to be rude, I opened my door and got into the car. As I started the engine and was about to leave, he tapped on the passenger window. "I want to show who the people were who died." Now he had my interest. The media seemed to have stopped paying attention to the actual lives that were lost. 9/11 had become two numbers that were overused. 9/11 this, 9/11 that, without any connection to the human beings who had suffered and died.

"Where did your husband work?"

"He was a firefighter."

"Would you want to talk about him?"

"I'm not sure. I would need to know more about this, but I really have to go." He asked me for my number and gave me his card. I did have a sense that he was sincere, so I gave him my number and went home.

When the phone rang that evening and a strange number came up, I almost did not answer. He was genuine on the phone and seemed to really want to make a film with heart that didn't exploit the victims. There was something about him that was trustworthy, and I felt in my gut that he was not out to do harm. I agreed to meet with him the next day.

The next morning, after speaking with him, I agreed to be in the documentary. I would be one of several women interviewed for their family stories. I liked the idea that people would know who Joey was. Maybe speaking about Joey would help to put the human beings who died back into 9/11. Even if I did not accomplish that, at the very least, people would know what it meant to me.

Being in this film was a great way for me to honor Joey. I wanted my appearance to be all about him and not about me. I never wore makeup, and I allowed myself to be filmed any time of day. If I had just woken up, and my eyes were puffy and I looked disgusting, I let the camera roll. I wanted Joey's life and death to matter. Ironically, talking about Joey all summer on film provided me with an escape from mourning him.

As the weeks rolled on, and I appeared in the film, I started to look forward to seeing Jack and talking about Joey. He and his cameraman were the only company I had during the day. After spending the past nine months grieving Joey every single day, it was nice to have a man to talk to. I developed a crush on him. He was a single, divorced father and what I liked about him the most was that he wanted me to talk about Joey. It was the perfect scenario. I could talk about my husband, who I was still madly in love with, to a guy who was not afraid to talk to me. When I spoke with him I could escape from my life. When the cameras were off, he talked to me like a friend, and I felt comfortable enough to tell him that I had a crush on him. He wanted to be my friend, and I was glad to have him as a one. It was good to know that it would never go further. As much as I liked him, deep down inside I knew that I was not ready for romance, even though I fantasized that I was. I knew my feelings for Jack were not real. I knew what love was, and I knew that this was not it. Still, it didn't seem to matter; it took me out of the hell I was living. I liked to hear about his life, and I liked that I could tell him about mine. Like a teenager, I became happy when I spoke to him and sad if I didn't. At times I hardly recognized myself. I felt like an addict and talking with Jack was my drug, the drug that could numb the pain I was in.

One evening, he called while I was with the boys in the living room. I left and went into the bathroom and locked the door. The boys were calling for me, but I did not answer. I did not want anything to interfere. I could hear them calling me while knocking on the bathroom door, but I stayed in my empty bathtub ignoring their calls. I knew that they could hear me. I felt like a very small person hiding from them, but I needed some fun, even if it was just for a few minutes.

It was bad enough that I was in pain, but to witness my boys' pain on a daily basis, made me feel inadequate as a mother. They were not able to put into words what they were feeling, but I knew what they yearned for. They wanted their father back, their family back, and the happy secure home they'd once had. Now they were left with a mother who could not make it all better. Sometimes it was unbearable for me to witness Sal's sadness. I struggled to get through the day, and they sensed it, and yet they clung to me. I could not understand if it was because they understood that I was all they had, or because I was a reminder of a vague memory of a happy life they once knew. In my dry bathtub I stayed on the phone to get away from them. I could hear them starting to cry on the other side of the door, but I didn't open it.

I was not good enough to be their mother. I was useless, and I was in pain, and I wanted to hide. I knew that I could never make their tears go away. Only Joey could. I continued to hide from them until I hung up. It might have been ten more minutes or ten seconds. It didn't matter. The guilt and shame I felt were tremendous.

Oddly enough, after I got off the phone, I did feel a bit renewed and uplifted, and I was able to give the boys more of me. I wiped away their tears and lied to them saying I did not hear them calling. I hated myself for lying, but what could I have said?

I was able to play with them and read to them because I felt a bit more balanced having had a conversation with an adult. Unfortunately, the feeling of equilibrium was not authentic. It was not coming from me. It was what I could borrow from the phone call. It was as if the crush provided me with a credit card, and I was using it for my drug—positive energy—but it only gave me a quick high because it wasn't real. And eventually it left me feeling like I was in debt emotionally.

Yet, even with the feeling of debt, I was grateful to the film, and the crush, because they got me through that first summer. As the season wound down, so did the crush. With the approach of autumn, I was finally able to see it for what it was, an escape. In the end, I netted a friend, and in regard to the film, a feeling of satisfaction. Appearing in the film, I accomplished my goal of honoring Joey.

Before the documentary was aired, it was shown at a local restaurant for all those who were in it, as well as their family and friends. It was a beautiful film about love and loss from the perspective of wives and mothers. To me the film succeeded in showing the emotional, human side of the two numbers: 9/11. It aired on the Oxygen network in September of 2002 and won a Gracie award.

After the insanity I felt from the crush, I knew that I had to find ways to build myself up from within. I wanted to be balanced so that I could be the mother that Sal and Vincent deserved.

September 11, 2002

I DID NOT WANT TO BE AT THE WORLD TRADE CENTER SITE
on the one year anniversary. I did not want to remember where
Joey died. I had a promise to keep—that after a year of mourning
I would move on. I had to keep my word. My plan was to return to
the church where we had been married. It was there that Joey had
put my ring on me, and it made sense to me that it would be the
place where I would take it off.

My morning started like any other. I dropped the boys off at
daycare. They did not need to be reminded of their dad's death.
They lived every day without him.

I had been giving a neighbor injections every day to keep her
blood from clotting, causing a miscarriage, so I headed for her house
next. As I got out of my car, I heard a radio. A man's car was parked
near the beach wall, and the door was open. The broadcast was live
from the World Trade Center. They were reading the names of
those lost there, and they were going in alphabetical order. When I
reached the steps to my neighbor's house, I heard "Joseph Agnello."
I knew I was meant to hear his name, and I was grateful to God for
letting me hear it. I knew that he would be with me that whole day,
and I felt him there with me at that moment.

After I had given my friend her injection I went home and got Joey's wedding ring out to take to the church. At that moment I wished I'd planned things better because I thought it would be nice if I could tie his ring and mine together with a white silk ribbon. I did not have one, and now I was not sure what I would use. I was about to leave the house when something made me turn around and head back to my room. I opened the top drawer of our dresser, which was a jewelry case drawer. I had been in and out of there daily; it was where I kept my watch and earrings. When I opened the drawer and looked down, there it was: a white silk ribbon. I had never seen it before. I had no idea where it had come from, but I knew it was a sign that I was doing what Joey wanted me to do. So I thanked God for it and I put it with Joey's ring.

After I entered St. Mark's Church in Sheepshead Bay, Brooklyn, I walked to the altar. There was one other person in the church and thankfully he was leaving and moving toward the main door. I was grateful because what I had to do was hard, and I did not want anyone to see me. I stepped up to the altar where Joey had put my wedding ring on me, and I shook and started to cry as I took it off. I always wore it—even through both pregnancies, even with my finger swollen. Where the ring had been, my finger had shrunk—out of proportion with the rest of my fingers. The medical term is atrophy. It was as if the ring had become part of me, and it felt strange not to have it on. I remembered a Mass I had gone to where the priest, talking about a widow who was having trouble moving on with her life, reminded us, "It's till death do you part." Trembling, I held my ring in my hand. It was no longer shiny like it had been the day Joey put in on my finger. It had scratches and marks that made it more beautiful to me. We had grown so much together as husband and wife in our years together, but I had to

193

move forward. As I stood there at the altar with tears pouring out of my eyes and snot coming out of my nose, I said a prayer and then took Joey's ring which matched mine exactly, although it was much larger, and I put my ring inside of his then took the white ribbon, tied a bow around them, and put them in my pocket. "See, Joey," I said in my head, "I kept my word about moving forward after a year. You know that I could never have taken that ring off unless you wanted me to."

I didn't want to leave the church, so I sat down in the front row and stared at the altar. I could see us up there at our wedding ceremony. We were smiling at each other. I could see into his eyes again. I could remember the pause when we got lost in each other's eyes after the deacon said, "You may now kiss your bride." It would never be erased. Never.

People were starting to enter the church, so I left. I wanted to be alone and I knew where I was headed.

There was hardly a soul on the beach. I walked all along the shore to the fence where Reese Park started, and then I walked back. It was a beautiful day, just like it had been a year ago—a lifetime ago.

I felt a sense of peace on this anniversary. Perhaps I had not done what looked right to others. I had not gone to the World Trade Center or to Joey's firehouse memorial. I had wanted to be alone so that I could be close to Joey, and I felt settled because I had followed my heart. I went home and got Chelsea and Durante and went back to the beach with them. I wanted them, too, to have something that would feel good. I let them off the leash and three of us ran down the beach. The dogs looked happy. They had suffered so much with Joey's death, but for now they were running free. I felt like Joey was there with us keeping the beach clear, because there was not a person or dog within miles, and this was just not the norm.

When we got closer to our block, I noticed a woman wearing a FDNY shirt. She had been sitting on the beach looking at the waves, and I could see that she was crying. I quickly took the dogs by the leash and walked toward the wall. I wanted to give her privacy. "You're Joe Agnello's widow, aren't you?" I was surprised she knew me.

"Yes," I answered.

She introduced herself. She was the sister of a firefighter, who was also killed on 9/11. We did not need to speak. We had never met, but we hugged each other for a few seconds and both cried.

"You couldn't go there either, huh?"

"No, Joey lived here and loved it here. This is where he is. Not down there."

"I agree," she said.

I walked home with the dogs and realized that it was like the whole day had been part of some divine plan. What were the chances that I would hear his name called? I had been at the right place at the right time, and I heard it at the beach wall, a place that Joey loved. Where did that white silk ribbon come from? I had never seen it before. Why was the beach so deserted on such a beautiful day? The dogs had not run that free since Joey was alive. I felt the tears run down my cheek. I was not alone.

Going Back to Work

IT HAD BEEN JUST OVER A YEAR SINCE I HAD WORKED AT THE hospital, and I missed working as a nurse. I realized that along with losing Joey, I had lost my career. I had been thinking about going back to work, but I was not sure I was ready. I was also a bit nervous, since it had been a year. I would be rusty and would need to renew some certifications.

One morning after I dropped the boys off at childcare, I found myself driving down the highway. I did not have a destination in mind, but I seemed to be driving into Manhattan. I found myself near the hospital, and I thought I would just drive by—I had not been there since September 9, 2001. I approached the Fifth Avenue entrance of the Women's Pavilion. I spotted an empty parking space. There were never spots available that time of day. I took it as a sign and parked the car. I would go in and say hello to my colleagues.

It felt strange to walk under the awning and up the stairs, which I had climbed so many times before. I felt like I had not been there in a lifetime. I was nervous as I pressed the elevator button. Part of me wanted to run back to my car, but there was no turning back now. When the elevator opened on the second floor, Labor and Delivery, I saw familiar faces of people I had worked with and was flooded with my own memories of Sal and Vincent's births, and of Joey. I quickly pushed them out of my mind so I wouldn't cry. When the elevator opened at the next floor, my heart started to race, I walked onto the unit. The clerk, from behind the desk, did a double take. "Oh my God, Vinnie!" She ran over and hugged me. Any nurses within an earshot came over and also hugged me. They were crying and that made me cry. I was not prepared for this emotional flood. I was no longer nervous, but happy I had gone in. The nurse manager of the unit came over and hugged me as well. She asked if I wanted to go to her office and talk. Once there, she told me that I still had my position if I wanted to come back. She kept my name on her list of per diem nurses, hoping that when I was ready I would return. "You could take a few classes, renew the things that have expired, and be back at work in a few weeks."

I wanted to return to my profession. I had been in a fog for a long time. I was concerned about the boys, though, and how I was going to handle their care. The hospital had changed to twelve-hour shifts in my absence. I would be away from them for so long. The nurse manager was flexible and said I could leave at three o'clock each afternoon. It looked good.

As I drove home, I sorted it out in my head: I'd need to hire a babysitter who could be at the house by five thirty in the morning. I would work a day or two during the week while the boys were in daycare most of the day. The babysitter could drop them off at eight a.m. and pick them up at three p.m. I could be home to have dinner with them, give them baths, and read them bedtime stories. It would work out well. It felt like it would be balanced. Having a part of my previous life back that had fulfilled me would make me a better mother to Sal and Vincent.

I was so happy with this new development. On the way home, I stopped by a uniform store and bought pretty scrub tops and new shoes. I could not wait to start working again and felt very optimistic about my life.

My first day of work started out feeling familiar. I woke at five o'clock in the morning and took a shower. In the early morning darkness, I felt strange getting dressed. I was alone. Usually Joey and I would whisper to each other. I no longer felt the security of knowing the kids would be in his hands. I started to worry about how the boys would react when I left them with the babysitter at six a.m. As much as they loved their father, they had often cried when I had left for work in the past.

Despite these reservations, I continued opening and closing drawers and the closet as quietly as I could. I did not want to wake the boys, but I did. As soon they were up, I was not only trying to get dressed and eat breakfast, I was also taking care of them and the dogs. I felt like a clumsy juggler. I knew that the babysitter would be there soon, though I really needed her now.

When she arrived promptly, I made my exit. As predicted, the boys cried and I explained that I would be back at dinnertime, but I could see the fear in Sal's eyes. His dad had gone to work and never come home. I was wondering if he was making that connection. Every part of my being wanted to stay with him but I also wanted to show him that I would be back. I wanted him to know that leaving didn't always mean forever. There was part of me that was afraid I could die in a car accident, the resulting reality hurting him even more, but I knew it was just crazy, worried thinking. I did feel that since I was alive it was because God had a sense of humor. I was the one who was afraid to have children and now I was a single mother. For some reason, it was supposed to be the three of us. Someone up there was getting a good laugh at my expense. I was pretty sure the joke that had become my life would continue.

As I drove to work, the sky filled with beautiful color. I had forgotten how peaceful the morning drive to work had been. I headed into the employee parking garage, but in doing so encountered some trouble making the turns up the ramps. It had been different when I drove our small Honda. Now I was in our van. I kept hitting the curbs. It was like trying to park a school bus. I hurried down the stairs and out into the streets of Manhattan. I loved walking on Fifth Avenue. As I neared the entrance of the hospital, I gazed toward Central Park. I loved that the park was so close. When my days were not busy, I had lunch there.

Arriving on the floor, it was like time stood still. Things were the same. I hugged more people whom I had not yet seen and started my day. When I walked into my first patient's room and introduced myself, I was cut off mid-sentence. Both my patient and her husband were smiling at me. "Vinnie, you were our nurse four years ago. We could never forget you." I had taken care of many mothers and babies over the years. Sometimes I would get the same patient a year or two later, but I couldn't remember this couple. The husband read my expression and spoke. "You don't remember us, do you? Maybe you will remember our daughter. She was born with a twisted foot." I still had no recall. The husband started to tell me how I had saved his daughter's foot. I have a really good memory, but I had no idea what this man was talking about. He explained: Four years before, when I had been their nurse, an orthopedic doctor had been in to see their baby. He had wrapped her foot, which was inverted, with a bandage.

Finally, the light bulb went off in my head. I remembered everything. I had gone into the room after the doctor had left. When I saw the baby's foot, it was turning blue. I told the parents it was not a good sign. The blood was being cut off and the foot was losing oxygen. When any body part loses oxygen for a period of time it can become necrotic, which causes damage to the tissues, sometimes irreversibly. Since the doctor had tied the bandage, I could not as a nurse go against his orders. The only thing I could do was call the doctor back to the room to check it. When the doctor came in, he was angry that I was questioning him. He didn't even look closely at the baby's foot. He was a young resident and, like some, had an attitude. He left saying it was fine. The parents were nervous, because it was their first baby and they were dealing with a deformity. They looked so confused. I went over to the baby, who was in the bassinet and the father followed me. I looked him in the eye and said the only thing that I could say as a nurse: "If this were my baby, I would loosen the bandage until her foot turns pink." The father looked at me. "Could you show me how?" I loosened the bandage and her tiny foot changed color from blue to pink. I was taking a big risk doing this, but I knew the young orthopedist was wrong. I treated the baby as if she were my own. I could never have lived with myself if I hadn't.

They both explained to me what had happened the following day. I had not worked that day so I had missed the rest of the story. The mother and daughter were about to be discharged when the same orthopedist came into their room. Again he wound the bandage tightly around the baby's foot. When they left, they felt uncomfortable because the baby's foot was turning blue again. They had an appointment that same day with a private orthopedist, but it would not be for several hours. What I had done was still in their memory. They called orthopedist's office and asked if they could bring the baby in right away. When the doctor saw the baby's foot, he quickly untied the bandage. The father explained to him that I had done the same thing the day before. The doctor said, "If you ever see that nurse again, thank her, because she saved your daughter's foot."

The story was incredible and a bit bizarre. The couple seemed normal. They had no reason to lie. It had never occurred to me that my actions as a nurse could have such a dramatic impact. How odd it was that on my first day back this woman would be one of my patients. What were the chances? I felt that I was meant to be there working as a nurse again. Any doubts about leaving the boys were erased.

The day was full of excitement for me, and I was happy to be there but I was also exhausted both emotionally and physically. I had not been on my feet like that in quite a while. In fact, I had blisters from my shoes, and I was a bit drained by answering questions about 9/11, but I was grateful for all of it. I felt a real sense of accomplishment as I left to go home.

In the parking garage, the attendant lit up as I went to pay. "I haven't seen you in a while!" It felt good to be recognized. It was almost as if nothing had changed. I just smiled, not wanting to explain.

"It's nice to be back." I paid and walked to my van. Making the turns out of the garage was again difficult. I wondered how I was going to deal with it. I was sorry I no longer had the Honda, but I'd known it would be too hard on the dogs. Reluctantly, I realized I was probably going to need a different car. This one was too big.

At a light, I called home to talk to the boys. I was looking forward to seeing them. I told them that I was on my way home and would be there to read them a story. I could hear the happiness in their voices.

I continued to work over the coming weeks and got into a bit of a routine. As it turned out, I traded the van for a car that would

VINNIECARLA AGNELLO

better fit the garage. I hadn't wanted to give up the van because it was higher off the ground than a car and gave me a good view. I felt safer driving the boys in it than in a lower vehicle. A colleague recommended getting an SUV. Many of the nurses had them. They fit easily in the garage, had height, and handled well in snow. It sounded like a good idea for work, but what about the boys? They were my world now, and they had to be safe. I did a lot of research into the SUVs on the market and found one with no incidences of rolling over. I traded in our minivan and got a new truck. I realized a new truck was one more piece of ammunition for people who were already judging me, but I felt good knowing I did what was right for the boys and me.

As predicted, some of my neighbors had plenty to say about a new truck. One by one they reported to me about how other people were talking about it. They failed to see that I was working again, or at least they said nothing to me about my re-entry into the workforce. They only saw a new truck.

While I was disappointed, I was not surprised. I had become accustomed to the fact that people only saw what they wanted to see. Instead, I set out to reclaim a part of the life I'd had prior to 9/11. I worked on and off for about a year. I kept at it hoping I could push away the dawning reality that even though I tried to act as if everything were the same as it had been, it wasn't, and neither was I.

It turned out that I was not really needed on my old unit, so I ended up working mainly on the sister unit one floor away. I was no longer working with my friends, and I did not have the same social interaction that I had enjoyed. The nurses on the new unit resented that I left at three p.m., while they, as staff nurses, were scheduled until seven p.m. As a per diem nurse, my schedule was more flexible. I was able to be there during the busiest time of the day and help with all the discharges, easing the burden for the other nurses, but the nurse manager did not need me past three p.m.

An even more unpleasant aspect of working on the sister unit was the wildfire way that rumors spread. They didn't know me, had seen my new SUV in the garage, and had read the papers. They made assumptions, and consequently there was never the camaraderie I had felt in pre-9/11 days on my old floor. On the outside I hid how much it hurt. I came to work with a smile, but I felt isolated, and quite honestly, I was not strong enough to deal with their negativity. The unit was not a positive environment, and positive was what I needed. In addition, no matter how upbeat I tried to be on workday mornings, the boys never got comfortable with me leaving. Their crying in the morning ripped my soul. It had been easier to leave when I knew they were with their father. They were not the same anymore. Sal looked okay on the outside, but he had changed. He was a serious kid now, not happy-go-lucky like he had been prior to losing his dad.

My love for being a nurse had not changed, but I realized that my children needed me more than my patients did. They needed all the love and time I could give them if they were ever going to heal. My career as nurse would have to wait. My calling now was to be the best mother I could be.

I Can See Clearly Now

IT WAS THE MIDDLE OF THE NIGHT AND I HEARD SAL CRYING.
My bedroom had changed shortly after 9/11. My queen-size bed now
had Sal's twin bed next to it. It was easier if Vincent slept in my bed
and Sal slept in a bed next to me. Then I could respond instantly to
their needs. After Joey died, Sal started having nightmares. Almost
once a week I would wake to his screams and wails. Vincent would
wake too, but when he saw that I was next to him, he would fall
back to sleep. Then I would roll over to Sal's bed and hold him until
he slept.

This night, though, Sal's cries were different. I could hear him
throwing up. And I could smell the feces. Reaching for my glasses,
I knocked them between the beds. All I could see was a blurry
outline of Sal in his bed. I could hear his distress. Where were my
glasses? I flailed blindly, but there was no time to search. So instead,
I reached out to the blur that was Sal. As I held him, he threw up on
my shoulder, and then I realized he had diarrhea, too. I could feel
it as it got on my pajamas and arm. Using the fuzzy outlines of the
room, and carrying Sal, I felt my way toward the bathroom. Now
we were both covered in feces and vomit. As I put Sal down in front
of the toilet, he continued to vomit. Still unable to see, I reached
toward the bathroom cabinet groping for my contact lenses. I put

one in one eye. I did not have time to put the other in, because now I could hear Vincent back in the bedroom vomiting. Leaving Sal standing in soiled pajamas in front of the toilet and navigating with one eye, I hurried back to the bedroom where Vincent was sitting up covered in vomit. I picked him up, and as I walked to the bathroom I felt something squishing between my toes. I had stepped in the diarrhea that had fallen from Sal. I ran the bath for the boys, took their pajamas off, and put them in the tub. Then I wrapped them in clean towels and got them clean pajamas.

They were burning up with fevers and were still crying from their ordeal. As fast as I could, I put clean pajamas on them and then put them down on the dog beds on the floor where it was actually clean. Finally I had a minute to put in my other contact lens which unfortunately provided a sharp image of the mess on the beds and on the floor. I wanted to cry. Instead, I ripped off my clothes, jumped into the shower, and, seconds later, in my terry cloth robe, I walked back into the bedroom only to be slapped with the stench of vomit and feces. I opened the windows and took the dirty sheets off the bed. I put them in a pile on the floor and then cleaned all around the floor coming across my glasses in the process. I really had to get that Lasik surgery Joey and I had always joked about. He always wanted to buy an old Corvette and fix it up, and I always wanted to get Lasik surgery to fix my miserable eyesight. "Get the car," I'd tell him. "Have the surgery," he'd respond. And then we would both decide to save the money for the boys' college. But, as I struggled to stretch clean sheets onto the beds and get the boys settled, I made up my mind. I was all these boys had and I had to be able to see to protect them. I would call around and get recommendations for a doctor as soon as things calmed down.

The boys were awake and feeling miserable—I'd hoped they would doze off while I cleaned the bedroom—so I tucked them in, turned on the TV, and slipped in one of their videos to distract them. As their glazed eyes followed the video, I raced the dirty sheets and soiled pajamas downstairs and washed them in the sink before putting them in the washing machine. I gagged as I stuck my hand in the dirty water to unclog the drain and throw the chunks of undigested food in the garbage. Then I hurried back upstairs to the boys. They were awake but getting drowsy. Again, diarrhea, this time Vincent. I held him in my arms. Managed to get him off the bed and to the bathroom without getting it on the sheets or the floor, but was unsuccessful in preventing it from reaching our clothes. I ran the bath again to clean off a crying Vincent and again I got him clean pajamas. I put him in my bed and then cleaned myself, my robe, and Vincent's pajamas. Once again, I returned to the room and put on clean pajamas. I sprayed some lemon spray and joined the boys in bed. By now it was around three o'clock in the morning. They were uncomfortable but were also exhausted, so they eventually fell back to sleep.

I, however, was wide awake. I thought about how scary it had been not being able to see. What if there had been a fire? How could I help them in an emergency? Joey had had perfect eyesight, but I was practically blind without my glasses. An enormous fear crawled up in my skin. My aloneness never felt bigger—I would be the one to handle all emergencies. I tried to fall back to sleep, but I was overwhelmed with trepidation. Eventually I drifted off but about an hour later, Vincent was crying. My day had begun. And I'd made a decision: even though it was a relatively new medical procedure, I would get Lasik surgery.

That morning I took the boys to the pediatrician. They had a virus, and all I could do was keep them hydrated and as comfortable as possible. That evening after I had put them to sleep, I went into the living room and collapsed on the couch. My house was a mess. I had not had time to clean it with the boys so sick. Now they were asleep and I finally had a moment. But no! There was Vincent's cry. Instead of heading toward him, I got up and went into the closet. I started crying and shaking my head, yelling at God: "You took the wrong parent, I can't do this alone, you know I was afraid of this. Why did you take him and not me?" I whipped my head back and forth so violently that I fell backwards into the coats hanging in the closet. Sitting on the closet floor, plopped into the middle of the coats, tears running down my cheeks, I continued screaming at God: "Do you need more proof you chose the wrong one? Look at me! I'm a mess. I'm blind! I'm tired! I'm so very tired of doing this alone!"

As I sat there in the black closet, Vincent's cries found their way to me. Louder this time, they pushed me to action. I went into the room and held him in my arms. I loved him so much. I wanted to make it better for him. I wished I was a better mother. I wished it had all never happened, 9/11, Joey's death. I did love the boys, but I felt like I was not enough. There was balance when it was the two of us. I missed my partner in crime. I thought about my breakdown in the closet as I held Vincent in my arms. What was wrong with me? How many more of these would I have?

I put Vincent to sleep in my bed, and then I got up and tiptoed out of the room. I did not want either of them to wake, so I didn't turn on the lights. Exhausted and with a feeling of sadness, I made my way through the darkened house to the kitchen, mumbling to Joey: "I wish you were here. I can't do this anymore alone. Where are you? I hate that you are gone. Did you see me in the closet like a crazy person? I could make mother of the year!" I started to cry again—and then it happened: singing, in the kitchen!

It startled me, but I knew it came from an old gag gift: a plastic fish that was glued to a wooden plaque. It was battery operated and was turned on by flipping a switch on the back of it. The fish's mouth would move and it would sing. We'd given it to the boys as a gift and whenever they played with it, they thought it was hilarious, but I hated the stupid thing and had hidden it on top of the refrigerator several weeks earlier so I wouldn't have to listen to it. There was no breeze that night that could have moved the fish, let alone switched it on. When it started singing, I knew it was Joey.

"Joey, you know I'm afraid of the dark," I hissed. "Stop it! You're freaking me out." The fish kept singing. "You know I'm a chicken shit . . . Okay, you're here. I get it. You are here. Now, please stop it!" Instantly, the fish stopped singing. The kitchen was still. The fish had not fallen. There was no wind. There were no clicks or sliding noises. Nothing but me and the dark. I knew it was him. He always made me laugh when I was frustrated or angry, and I did smile and stop crying that night, despite myself.

When I found my way back to bed, the boys were sleeping peacefully. Soon after, so was I.

Not Alone

I TOLD PEOPLE WHOM I COULD TRUST ABOUT THE TIMES I felt Joey around me. Whether they doubted me or not, they were supportive. One night on the phone with my aunt Linda, she said if I asked Joey for signs, he would give them to me. I decided to try it. The first sign I asked for was wild horses, because of Joey's joke about being a stallion. "If you are okay," I said to him, "let me see wild horses running." It was not common in my world to see wild, running horses, so if I saw them, I knew it would be from Joey. I put on PBS to watch Masterpiece Theater, and Ralph Lauren had donated money to support it. There on the television were wild horses running. The announcer said: "The world of Ralph Lauren." It was Joey.

I was so impressed by his spirit that I asked him to show me another sign. I picked something out of the ordinary. I had never read *Little Red Riding Hood* to the boys. They had no reference to it, so I asked Joey to let me hear someone say, "Little Red Riding Hood."

I had told my in-laws that I would bring the boys over to see them the following week. I was a bit nervous about it. My relationship with them had been strained since Joey's death. We seemed to let our grief divide us. We were all hurting, and there was anger in losing Joey that we shared. We tried to understand each other, but we were all in so much pain that it was hard.

For me, the simple act of going to their house was difficult, because of the pictures of Joey they kept everywhere. It made me so sad to see how much they missed him, and seeing all those pictures made my own feelings flare, too, but I took the boys that day so they could see their grandparents and so their grandparents could see them. I hid my pain and put on a smile for my in-laws and for the boys. I wanted the visit to be positive, and it was.

My father-in-law played basketball with the boys with a plastic hoop that he had hung on a door. They were too little to reach the hoop, so he picked them up and let them throw the ball in. This made them screech with delight. When it was time to eat, we all sat down to a lunch of spaghetti and chicken cutlets, a meal Joey loved. My mother-in-law is an amazing cook, and the boys gobbled up the food. Being silly, Sal pretended to be a dog. He put his face to his plate and picked up a chicken cutlet with his mouth. Vincent laughed. "Who does he think he is? Little Red Riding Hood?"

I could hardly believe what I was hearing. Vincent's words didn't even make sense. Sal was shaking a cutlet back and forth, like a dog does with a toy. Saying Little Red Riding Hood had nothing to do with Sal's action. I was sure it was Joey. I felt a sense of validation. He was there with all of us.

About a week later, the boys and I and my neighbor Susan and her son were driving home from the Children's Museum on Long Island. We had exited the Meadowbrook Parkway and were headed south on the Southern State Parkway. There were two cars pulled onto a grassy area on the middle divider of the highway ahead of us. I slowed down. As I got closer I could see a dog stuck on the median. I pulled over.

Instantly, I remembered Joey pulling back into our driveway a short twenty minutes after leaving with the boys for Trader Joe's the spring before he died. "Sorry we're back so soon," he said, "but look what I found." He grinned and I peered into the back of the van. He'd been almost out of Rockaway when he'd seen the boxer running loose by the side of the road. He was afraid a car would hit it, so he stopped and called to the dog. The dog happily ran to him and jumped into the van. Clearly, it had been abandoned; his ribs stood out. It looked like he hadn't eaten in weeks.

We'd gotten the dog out of the van and put him in the backyard, then gave him some food and water. We wanted to keep him, but our house was too full. We already had Chelsea and Durante. Instead we decided to personally find him a good home. It didn't take long. Within an hour, our neighbor Mike had taken the dog and given him to his brother—a loving home. That's just how we were with animals. We loved them, and never hesitated to help an animal in need.

This dog on the median strip was a Rottweiler, and it looked frightened and skittish. I peered through the windshield charting the scene. One man was trying to get the dog to come to him, but it was too scared. The guy gave up as I sat there, and drove away. A woman pulled over and tried to get the dog to come to her, but she wasn't having any luck either. I got out and called the dog, but it wouldn't come to me, and at one point we got too close and the dog almost ran into traffic. I had to do something. While the other woman gave up and got in her car and left, I called the police. A state trooper came within five minutes.

My neighbor Susan wanted to go once he arrived, but I wanted to stay and make sure the dog would be safe. I told the trooper the dog was afraid of people and that he had to stop the traffic in order to get the dog to safety. He tried to get the dog to come to him and the dog once again almost ran into traffic. The trooper said he would close the westbound traffic. We were on the westbound side. I told him he had to close down both sides of the highway.

"There is no way I am going to do that, ma'am."

I pleaded.

While he and I talked, an animal control car pulled over. The man was going to take the dog to safety. I told him that he should not take a step toward the dog until both sides of the highway were closed. Again, the trooper said he would not do that.

"You have to! Just think of how dangerous it will be for drivers on both sides of the highway when that dog runs into the road. It could cause an accident. People could die!" I told the trooper I was not going to allow innocent people or a dog to be killed.

He stared at me for a long minute. "You should go," he said.

I felt bold. I told the trooper I would go when the dog was safe. He looked angry, but I was not backing down.

"Let me see your license."

I reached for my wallet. It was a special one for me, a gift from the Fire Officers union. Inside it had a gold badge engraved with the words: Line of duty widow: Lt. Joseph Agnello. As I handed him my license, he glimpsed the badge. He asked if he could see it. He studied it then said, "Mrs. Agnello, I am so sorry for your loss. You can stay here. I'll call for another trooper. We'll close down both sides of the highway and get the dog out of harm's way."

I was a bit shocked, but then I knew that Joey was with me. The other trooper showed up on the other side. Together they completely shut down the highway. The animal control officer walked toward the dog, which ran first onto the eastbound side and then onto the westbound side, and then onto a nearby road. The animal control officer jumped into his car and followed the dog. I prayed it would be okay.

Before the trooper reopened the westbound side of the parkway, he let me get back on the road. I thanked him and drove home. I was grateful to the badge and to Joey, who even in death was there for me.

Chelsea and Durante

OUR BOXERS, CHELSEA AND DURANTE, WERE HAVING A HARD time coping with our new life. When Joey was alive, days had been much quieter, but now there were babysitters coming and going and neighbors in our house. For the dogs, it added up to more chaos and less routine, which threatened and stressed Durante, especially. Even when Joey was alive, Durante was known to be aggressive, but we had dealt with it by giving him long walks and lots of playtime. That had all changed. While I took the dogs on long walks when the boys were at daycare, in the evenings and on weekends, I couldn't get the time. I let them out in our small backyard, but that was not enough, and they simply did not get much affection from me anymore. Any energy I could muster went to the boys, who were needier now. I loved the dogs, but the fact was that it was impossible for them to have the life they had known before.

Without Joey as his leader, Durante's instincts put him on high alert. He became very protective of all of us, especially the boys. One day when my neighbor was walking him, he bit someone. Thank God it was just a nip, but I feared that it could get worse given our circumstances. I always put him in our backyard whenever someone came to the house. One afternoon a friend stopped by. I put Durante in the backyard, but unbeknownst to me, the babysitter let him back in. She did not realize my friend was there—so many people in and out.

Before she stopped by, my friend had cleaned blood from an injury to her dog's paw, so she had the scent of that blood on her hands. When she bent over to pick Vincent up, suddenly there was Durante lunging to protect him. He bit her face. It was a nightmare. She ended up being fine, but it could have been really bad.

Joan came over later and gave me the hard truth. She said that Durante couldn't be controlled and should be put to sleep before he really hurt someone. I was horrified by her suggestion. Durante was like my child. He was a member of our family. How could I ever put him to sleep?

My mind went spastic: I felt so bad for my friend, I knew it could happen again, I didn't want him to hurt anyone, I just wanted Durante to have a happy life again. Should I give him away? I couldn't end his life. I knew he couldn't live with us anymore, and I was sick with the thought of losing another member of my family.

Because I was paranoid about someone coming and taking him away, I called the firehouse and asked if Durante could spend the night there while I found him a home. I was honest about the fact that he had bitten someone, but I told them he was a great dog. He just needed more time and attention. Someone would see that and give him a home, wouldn't they? I took him to the firehouse that night, where I felt he would be safe. I was hoping some single firefighter, with no children, might fall in love with him and give him a home. When I drove away I cried all the way home as I thought about the look in his eyes and how confused he was about being there. I told the guys to ask everyone they knew if they would take him and give him a home. I offered to pay for all of his food and vet care for the rest of his life.

When I got home that night, I did not sleep at all. I cried and prayed that Durante would be okay and that someone would love him and give him a good home. The next morning when I called the firehouse, no one had been able to find him a home. No one wanted a dog that was known to be aggressive. I called shelters that did not destroy dogs, but none would take a known biter.

When I got to the firehouse, Durante ran to me, so happy to see me. When I took him outside he peed for it seemed like minutes; he had been so nervous. I had nowhere to take him. No one wanted him. I felt shaky, like I could throw up. I had to do the thing that I had feared the most to a dog that I loved with all my heart and soul. I had no choice but to take Durante to a vet to be euthanized. I knew that if I didn't do it at that moment, I would never be able to. I wanted to be with him, so that he would not be scared. I wanted him to know that he was loved and for his last moments to be with me by his side petting him. The guys in the firehouse called the vet around the corner and told him about Durante. The vet said that I could bring him in right away. I stayed with Durante, kissing his head and petting him, and telling him that I loved him until he was gone. I took his collar and his leash with me and signed papers to have him cremated. They would send me his remains. I felt sick and cried the whole way home. I thought of Joey on the other side waiting for Durante and tried to comfort myself with that thought. Durante would finally understand that Joey had not left him on purpose and that he loved him.

When I got home, I could not function. All I could do was go to bed and cry. I felt like I had killed my own flesh and blood. It was different than the pain I felt in losing Joey. I felt like a mother who failed to protect her child from harm. It was at that moment that I finally had a new understanding of the pain that Joey's mother was going through. I called her and told her about Durante and told her how sorry I was that she had lost her son, how I was sorry that I in my own pain as his wife I had not been able to understand hers. It was the truth.

As the weeks passed, the only thing that gave me any sort of relief was the thought of Joey and Durante together again, taking long walks in paradise.

I still had Chelsea and tried to give her more attention. I was concerned about how she would react to losing Durante. After Joey had died, Chelsea had started having seizures. While Joey was alive, she had suffered from them in times of stress—brought on by thunderstorms or the sounds of fireworks—but he had always been there to pick her up and comfort her. After he died she seemed to have the seizures more frequently, and they seemed to come out of nowhere.

One day early in our time alone, I had taken her down to the beach. I was with the boys and she was running in the water. She liked to play in the waves. Suddenly, she dropped down and had a seizure at the shoreline. The water was coming up. She rolled back and forth as the water hit her. She couldn't control her movements. I ran to her and pulled with all my might to get her away from the water. It was scary because I had to leave the boys and attend to her quickly. After I got her away from the water, she was too weak to move. She weighed about eighty pounds, and I did not have the strength to pick her up. I had to wait until she was ready to walk back home, but she really needed to be carried. I took her to the vet after that and was told she should be on medication to stop the seizures. The vet also said she had a heart problem and could die any day. I tumbled into shock. I had just lost Joey and Durante. Now Chelsea? I drove home with her that day knowing I would not put her on the medication. There were too many side effects. I would find a more natural way to help her. Soon thereafter I took her to my chiropractor's wife, who was a practicing chiropractor for racehorses. She helped Chelsea a great deal. With adjustments, Chelsea rarely had seizures and her quality of life improved. I was grateful we had access to that kind of chiropractic care, but even with that blessing, there were things that no amount of intervention could heal.

After Durante died, I could see it in her eyes—she was missing him. Durante had been her puppy, and as long as he was alive they were together. It was hard for her to lose Joey, and now she had lost her son.

Three months after Durante's death, I was in my room watching a movie, and I felt Joey's presence. It was like he was looking in on me from the bedroom doorway. I could feel his energy. I looked over to the door and quietly said, "Hi, Joey. Why are you here?" He had a way of showing up whenever I was in a crisis. I was a bit confused about why he had shown up at this time, because everything was okay. I had been lost in the movie when I first felt him. It was almost as if he had just popped by to say hello, because shortly after that he left. I slid back out of my life and into the story on screen. There was a noise out in the living room about that time, but I did not get out of bed. I was comfortable. I would deal with whatever had fallen in the morning.

My neighbor, who was kind enough to walk Chelsea arrived. I heard him come into the house. He was softly calling for Chelsea. I heard him walk into the living room. "Vinnie," he called. "I think Chelsea is dead." I leaped from bed and found my neighbor. There was Chelsea lying on the floor. I bent down to look closely. He was right. She was gone. I felt sick when I realized that the noise I had heard was Chelsea falling to the floor. I cried when I saw her face and felt sad that she had died alone. Then I thought about Joey's presence. Oh God, he had been here to take her with him!

I was comforted to know that she was not alone, but I also felt like I had failed her. That evening when I had been eating with the boys, she had kept licking my hand. At the time, I could not dote on her and give her the attention she was looking for. I felt bad that I did not get to kiss or hug her one last time. The only thing that gave me comfort was the fact that I knew for sure that she was with Joey. I kept picturing all three of them together again and I felt better knowing that at last she knew how much Joey loved her.

My neighbor carried her out and put her in his garage so that the boys would not have to see her. I prayed that she would now understand what had happened to our life. I also wanted her to know that she was our first baby, the first one we gave all our love to. She was part of the beginning of our marriage, and she would always have a special place in my heart. I would always love her.

The next morning I had to tell the boys about Chelsea. Sal kept asking where she was. I told him that her body was in the garage and that her soul was free and with his daddy and Durante.

"I want to see Chelsea."

I told him we would go to the garage after breakfast.

"Can we see her now?"

I said we would go once we were finished having breakfast.

"Can we go see her now?"

Sal was four and a half. He knew that death meant you never came back, but he had never seen what it looked like. It was like he was trying to understand it.

When we went to see Chelsea, Sal didn't cry. He just stared at her. He seemed to understand that she was not sleeping. I think it helped him to understand about his dad.

The Disney Cruise and the Mother I Was

WITH THE DOGS GONE, WE HAD MORE FREEDOM TO TRAVEL. I hated staying home, so whenever I could leave, I did. I left our home with its painful memories. On the weekends, I went to my mother's house and saw my friend Victoria. Without the dogs, there was no reason to hurry home. As long as the boys were with me, we could stay away as long as we liked.

It had been a cold and miserable winter made more sad by Chelsea's death. I felt that the boys and I could use a bit of sunshine and warm air. Being such a big fan of Disney, I decided to try one of their cruises. It was kid friendly so I knew they would do a great job keeping the boys entertained. I chose a four-day trip to the Bahamas. After my "spring break-out," a year before, I was confident to travel with the boys on my own. I had it down to a science. I put them in the double stroller, checked our bags on our arrival to the airport, and checked the stroller at the gate. We sat together in one row in the plane. I gave them juice so their ears didn't bother them. I flew on JetBlue. They had the best flight attendants and TV. The boys ate snacks and watched Nick Jr. videos the entire flight. I planned to end the trip at Disney World, after the cruise. The boys were older and they could enjoy it more. If I needed it, they had the best childcare available. I could not foresee any problems . . . unless the boys got sick again.

As soon as we boarded the ship, it felt like we were on vacation. Our bags were already in our cabin; it was warm and sunny. We changed into our bathing suits and jumped into the pool right away. There was plenty of food available nearby and the boys had fun splashing and swimming. All three of us played there most of the day.

The next day the ship was due to go to Disney's private island, Castaway Cay. I was looking forward to it because the boys loved the beach. That night after a delicious dinner and a show, we went to bed. I had been sleeping for a couple of hours when I woke up with a pain in my head and stomach. I threw up in the bathroom and spent most of the night there with diarrhea and vomiting. I remembered how Joey had held my forehead and kept my hair back when I vomited during both pregnancies. It would have been nice to have him there with me. I was weak and burning up with a fever caused by the bug the boys had just recovered from. After I had vomited for what felt like a year, I went back to sleep.

I woke up to the boys jumping on my bed. "Mommy, Mommy, look at the island!" They were pointing out the glass door to the veranda. Shaking and limp with fever, I struggled out of bed. No way could I take care of the boys in my condition. I called for room service, which came free with the cruise. The boys ate breakfast. I put the television on to keep them entertained while I went back to sleep. It was around ten thirty in the morning when I decided to get dressed and take them to the childcare facility. Since we were now docked, they had moved childcare to the island. I was relieved to know that the boys would be able to play and swim on the beach while I went back to the room to sleep. Shaky, with a throbbing head, I took what felt like the longest walk I had ever taken to childcare.

As it turned out, the childcare area activities did not include swimming and it was not near the water. Well, at least the boys were outside. The area was in the shade so they would be out of the sun.

When I got back to the room, it was eleven thirty a.m. I passed out and woke two hours later, still weak, but my fever was down a bit. I had no appetite and could not stop thinking about the boys and how they deserved to go to the beach. Even though I still felt horrible, I put on my bathing suit. *I* would take them swimming.

They were so excited to see me. As I walked with the boys to the beach, Vincent fell asleep in his stroller. I could not take the stroller on the beach, so I picked him up and held him in my arms. We walked on, across the sand toward the water. Sal stopped, wet his feet, and said he wanted to go in. I told him to stay exactly where he was. I wanted to put Vincent down in a spot where I could keep my eyes on him. The problem was that the spots near the water were already taken. I finally found a shady place, which was close enough to where Sal and I would be. When I turned around, he was gone.

My heart pounded. I was still holding Vincent in my arms as I started to walk back to where Sal had been. Frantically I scanned the water. No Sal. I started to panic. What if he'd drowned and no one had noticed? I squinted, scanning back and forth, in all directions, but I could not see him. "Sal!" I yelled, my voice cracking. "SAL!" It came out as a universal maternal distress sound, because suddenly all the mothers in earshot were gathered around me. "What does he look like?" one asked. She was going to look in the water. As I described him, tears ran down my face. I yelled louder. Another mother offered to hold Vincent, who miraculously was still sleeping. I had no other choice; I had to move faster to find Sal and I could not do that with Vincent in my arms. I did not worry about handing him over in front of so many mother witnesses.

Far away I saw a tiny child who looked like Sal, walking with a lifeguard in our direction. I held my breath. When I saw that it was Sal, I ran as fast as I could, adrenaline pumping.

After I had recovered him, I was too drained to take him swimming. It would be better if we went back on the boat. We walked back to the pavement, but with Vincent in my arms I had trouble getting the stroller to stand up. It kept falling. People walked by. No one offered to help. Finally Sal picked up the stroller so that I could put Vincent in it. I was fighting tears. I just wanted to get out of there and back to the ship where I felt safe. We had to board a tram. I had to fold the stroller. I struggled again. Would this be the proverbial straw that broke the camel's back? Suddenly a woman stepped in to help and I felt a surge of relief. Soon we would be on the ship. I would let the boys play in the baby pool and I would rest on a chaise lounge.

Gone was my confidence about traveling solo. When we got to the pool, it was closed. The boys were hungry so I got them lunch and we returned to the room. As they ate, I lay down and tried to rest. My mind retraced the old familiar ground: Why did I bother to take them on vacations? I hated that I needed to take them to places that were family friendly, but I needed locations geared for small children. It was so hard to be surrounded by happy families. When I saw couples having a good time with their children, it made me feel sad. Seeing any father playing with his children made my heart ache for Sal and Vincent. I closed my eyes and tried not to focus on how much I missed Joey. I felt so vulnerable and sorry for myself that he was not there to take care of the boys or me. I prayed that I would feel better and finally drifted off to sleep.

When I woke, my fever was gone. I took the boys back to the pool, which was now open and they swam and had a good time. It was our last night and, feeling better, I took the boys to the farewell show. The show was about families taking a cruise together, specifically highlighting the bond between couples as they vacationed with their children. I didn't know whether to laugh or cry.

When we got home, I told everyone all the bad things that had happened on the cruise. They all agreed it sounded like hell. When I went to a therapy session, I expected another sympathetic ear, but I got something far better.

After I told my story, my therapist, Leslie, smiled and said. "What a great opportunity this was for you to see the mother that you are." I didn't really understand. She explained. "You were sick and had a fever and had every right to rest but you got up and tried to give your boys a day at the beach. Can you see what kind of mother you are?" I was surprised. I never looked at it in any way other than being a victim in the midst of a disaster. I was grateful to Leslie for seeing outside of the box. She was able to show me the bigger picture and help me rethink my attitude. She called it the gift in the situation. Perhaps I was a better and stronger mother than I had thought. Perhaps the cruise had been more than just one bad thing after another. Maybe, just maybe, I was going to be all right as a single mom.

Boobs

"Oh my god! What the hell happened to your boobs? They look like dried apricots!"

"I know. It's because I just stopped breast-feeding. I'm hoping they will return to normal soon."

I was with my mother trying on bathing suits at Lord & Taylor, my mother's favorite place to be. She had not breast-fed, so the comment didn't bother me—she had never seen breasts like this before—and I was used to her honesty, but she was right about the breasts. They did look bad. It had to be temporary. They had to snap back into place, right?

When I drove home that day, I thought about how I looked naked. It was not a pretty sight. In the three weeks that Joey was missing, I had lost fifteen pounds, and I still had not gained it back. I had lost my appetite the first six months and now I was consciously watching what I ate. It was bad enough that I was widow. I didn't want to be a fat one. And I was working out, mainly to combat depression. Given all that, you'd think the mirror would reflect a healthy looking body. Instead my body just looked awful.

In addition to the pendulums on my chest, I had a bump where my flat stomach used to be. It was from the C-section. No matter how much I exercised, that was not going away. The doctor had pulled my muscles to the side to get Sal out, and just like the breasts, the stomach muscles had not snapped back into place. It was so unfair. I was thirty-five, but my body looked and felt much older.

As I drove, I remembered where I had seen breasts that looked like mine. They were on one of my patients from years ago. She was a nice lady in her eighties who had just had a hysterectomy. At the beginning of my shift, I admitted her to our floor. She had just come out of the recovery room. It was around three thirty in the afternoon. She was as sweet as she could be. I made sure that she was in the bed comfortably, and then I assessed her condition. I oriented her to the room and to her call bell and introduced myself. She was sharp and understood everything I said, and she kept calling me dear. I told her to rest and that if she needed me, to use the call bell. It was autumn and the days were short. It was dark outside when I returned to her room to change her IV. The same sweet old lady, whom I had left an hour before lying in bed was now standing on the bed naked. She was ripping the IV out of her arm and blood was squirting out all over the place. "Stay the fuck away from me," she yelled. She was so thin and wrinkled that her skin hung loosely on her body, and her boobs, which hung like two long deflated balloons almost down to her knees, were swaying back and forth. She had sundowned, which sometimes happens to elderly patients. They lose their orientation when it gets dark outside.

I could never get that image of her standing on the bed out of my mind, her naked, skinny body and her swaying breasts.

When I got home that night and was putting on my pajamas, I felt assaulted by my own image in the mirror. Emotionally I felt like damaged goods, and now my body was looking the same way. I thought about what Joey had said one night after I had just breast-fed Vincent. "Maybe you should get them lifted when you close up shop."

"Sure thing, if you want to spend the money on it." Then we both smiled knowingly, because Joey was very careful with money, and besides it came with the family package. We had children together; my body changed, but we got two healthy babies in the process. My sagging boobs were just part of the price we paid, along with sleep deprivation.

I never thought about my body while breast-feeding. It was all about what was best for the babies, and I had been an incredible producer of milk. I went from beautiful *B*s to triple *D*s with milk, and now they hardly qualified as *A*s. While Joey was alive, my boobs still looked great. Now when I looked in the mirror, all the effects of stress and time were evident. I literally had to scoop my boobs up in order to fit them into my bra. There were times when they would slip out and hang underneath it. Even my girlfriends noticed the change—so I knew it wasn't just me being critical of my body. Victoria, Denise, and Kelly had all seen my boobs, and they'd had the same horrified look on their faces. Yes, ladies, this is what I got from breast-feeding for three straight years. Not one of them said they looked fine and that I was being critical. It was hard to feel good about what looked like two hanging gym socks, but what bothered me the most was that the man who loved me and would have remembered my beautiful twenty-something breasts was now gone. I felt bad. I looked bad. And I wanted to feel better.

Because Joey had died in the line of duty, and the boys would receive scholarships, I felt I could use some of our savings and fix my body. I had an option. I had judged women who got plastic surgery, and here I was considering it—oh, how a life can change.

I scheduled an appointment with Dr. Robert Freund. I was referred to him by my dermatologist. He was compassionate and professional and very talented. He told me I had severe ptosis—the medical name for sagging. I was a bit relieved to know there was a name for it. I felt validated; my deformity had a name! He gave me a breast lift, using the smallest implants that they made, and a tummy tuck. It turns out that most women who get breast augmentations are women post childbirth and not twenty-year-olds looking to be the next Dolly Parton. I was so grateful to Dr. Freund and to his wonderful staff. I was still young, and now I looked that way, too.

I was not the only one to notice. When Joey had been missing, Sal had returned to my breast. It made him feel secure. It was not a big deal, but it was hard to have both boys there. After Joey's funeral I had decided to wean both of them. It was easier for Vincent because he had his binky, but Sal needed an explanation. So on the last day I fed them, I showed him my sagging breast that had just been emptied of milk. "See, Sal, the milk's gone."

"Oh, Mommy, you are right. The milk is gone." It was that easy. He could see that it was gone, and he was fine with it.

About a month after my surgery, I was getting dressed in my room and Sal walked in. "Mommy, Mommy! Look!" He was pointing at my breasts and smiling. "The milk's back!"

I chuckled. "It's not milk, Sal." I was grateful they looked natural.

All Roads Lead to Manhattan

IN JUNE OF 2001, I HAD TOLD JOEY ABOUT A WRITING COURSE I wanted to take that fall. It was part of NYU's continuing education department. Since Joey had been studying to take his second FDNY promotion test, and since it was more important that he take that test than it was for me to take the course, I'd decided to wait until January when it would be offered again. Joey would have the time then to watch the boys.

I never took that course, but after I started working again at the hospital, I was reminded about it by a nurse friend. I still wanted to write and now, unfortunately, I had a lot to write about. I found a class that met during the week. It was perfect because the boys were in daycare. It was on Tuesdays at the New School in Manhattan.

The other students in the class were all adults from different walks of life. Our instructor told us to write from our hearts, and we did. I loved hearing the stories that the others wrote, and when I shared my own, I liked the feedback. I knew that I had a lot of feelings inside that I wanted to write about. I thought that writing might help me heal. The class was helping me to have the confidence to write and to share my stories. My goal was to write a book. As I wrote my stories, I sensed that I still had so much to experience before I could write a book. It felt good, though, to know I had a place to start and a direction to go. Even if it took years, I felt as if I could do it, and that someday I would.

I loved my New School class, and I loved being in Manhattan. The more time I spent there, the more I wanted to live there. This came as a surprise to me, because I never thought I would want to leave my life by the beach. I had always loved living in Belle Harbor. I loved everything about it when Joey was alive. It was out of the way, and not many people even knew it existed. It was part of New York City, and yet it felt like another world. It was physically beautiful, and I especially loved the beach in wintertime. I loved walking with the dogs in the snow down by the dunes in Fort Tilden and then coming home to our warm cozy home. But everything I had loved about living by the ocean in our quiet and beautiful neighborhood now made me sad.

My home now felt like a stark and lonely place. Seeing the houses lit up at night with families inside and lives going on made me feel left out. I came to hate being in our home without Joey. Everything we had created together just stared me in the face. I had heard that some widows with young children had sold their homes and moved. I was starting to see why.

I was desperately searching for life. As I found myself in Manhattan more and more, I discovered and loved that it had a life of its own. When I was in Manhattan, I felt like there was hope. I loved that there were people everywhere. There was an energy I could feel. And I could just get lost there, be just another face in the crowd where no one knew who I was or anything about me.

On Saturday mornings I took the boys to Manhattan for swimming lessons. I felt optimistic when we were there. I often stayed after their classes and took them to museums and to Central Park. The more time I spent there, the more I wished we could live there. We could easily come and go without anyone watching or judging. We could go to museums, Broadway shows, galleries, parks, the zoo. Getting around would take minutes instead of the hour or more of commuting by car. Everything about Manhattan appealed to me. It would be where I could start a new life, different than the one before, away from the pain and the constant reminders of the life that I had loved.

I wanted to move there more than anything, but it was too expensive. Maybe I could find an apartment in Park Slope, Brooklyn. It was just a few subway stops from Manhattan. I looked at apartments there, but they were just as expensive as Manhattan.

My dream seemed so out of reach. So I found myself spending a lot of time actually living in Manhattan and sleeping in Belle Harbor. It felt right that we should live there, and one day we would. When the time was right, the door would open.

Do not go where the path may lead,
go instead where there is no path and leave a trail.
—Ralph Waldo Emerson

Part Three

The Power of Love

Life as a Single Woman

DURING THAT FIRST WINTER AFTER WE'D LOST JOEY, A CLOSE
friend of mine had gone through a divorce and she had returned
to the nightclub circuit. She wanted to meet men. One night she
invited me to go with her, but I had no desire to go to a nightclub.
She was in a different place than I was emotionally. Although I loved
to go dancing when I was young and single, it seemed ridiculous to
me that I should go out while I was still breast-feeding. I could just
see a man asking if I wanted a drink. "No thanks. I'm lactating."

Six months later that friend had met and was dating a man, and
I was still continuing with my marriage, although I was starting to
realize why the vow says, "Till death do you part." A healthy and
happy marriage really does require two live people. My marriage
with my dead husband was disappointing to say the least. I could
usually keep myself distracted with the boys in the evening, but
then would find myself crying late in the night.

I was in my bed when the phone rang. I had been having a
hard day missing Joey and was starting to cry. Before I picked up
the receiver I took a breath, wiped my cheeks, and tried to sound
normal. It was Jack, the filmmaker. After my mad crush, we'd ended
up being friends, and he and I would talk occasionally.

"Crying again?" he asked. "You have to stop. You have to get out of your house."

I mumbled a weak excuse.

"I'm getting together with some friends," he continued. "Come out. You will feel better."

"It's cold and raining. I'm not up to driving into Manhattan. Besides I'm in my pajamas."

"Vinnie, it's six o'clock. Are you kidding me? Get dressed and get here."

"I'm not sure I can get a sitter."

"You can get a sitter. I'm not going to let you cry over Joey and feel sorry for yourself. Come on! Get dressed and call me when you're ready. I'll tell you how to get here."

He hung up before I could say no again. I thought about it. Maybe I should go out and spend time with adults. It would be a nice change from watching a movie and crying. I decided to get dressed and go.

I cried as I drove. It was dark, cold, and rainy, and the weather seemed to mirror my emotions. I was no longer crying over Joey, but I was reflecting on my life: I was lonely and sad all the time, and I had started to become comfortable with misery. I knew that this was not at all what Joey had wanted for me and that I had failed to keep my promise to him about moving on. But staying put was easy and safe. As I listened to the rhythm of the windshield wipers, I reconciled that going out in this dismal weather was a good step in moving on. As I got close to the city I could see the skyline and I felt a sense of optimism. It looked beautiful even without the two towers. I got to the restaurant and made sure there was no evidence of tears on my face before I walked in. I was revived by the cold air and already felt that I was in the right place.

Jack and his friends were by the bar, waiting for a table. I joined them. They were friendly and made me feel welcome. When we got to the table and were ordering food, Robert, a friend of Jack's, showed up. He was with his cousin John. Robert sat down next to Jack, and John saw that there was room next to me, so he took a seat. Robert and Jack started talking and laughing. John and I sat there awkwardly for a moment, but then started talking to each other.

John mentioned that he had seen me in the documentary and knew who I was. He seemed like a nice guy, and we talked easily to each other. We were in the same place emotionally. He had been separated from his wife for about as long as I had been widowed. When we started talking, it was as if everyone else faded away and it was just the two of us sharing our war stories of loneliness. At one point I felt like he was coming on to me, and I was a bit uncomfortable, but I did like his company. We continued to talk as the others continued their own conversations.

At the end of dinner, Jack and his friends left, and John and I were the only two there. I enjoyed his company for a while longer, but then I felt it was time to go home. He walked me to my car and he asked if I wanted to go out sometime. I said that I was not ready to go out on a date, but that we could be friends. In the weeks that followed, he called me almost every day, and we always had something to talk about. I started to look forward to his calls. It was nice to have a man interested in me, but I was still not looking to date anyone. Eventually he did convince me to meet him for dinner. I was full of ambiguity.

I agreed to go to dinner as friends. I agreed to meet John at the restaurant. If he picked me up it would feel too much like a date. As I drove to the restaurant, I felt sick at the idea of meeting John there and not Joey. While I was parking, John called to tell me that he was inside at the bar. He would be looking for me when I came through the door. I got out of my car and walked to the door of the restaurant and then stopped. I stood there unable to move. Thoughts flooded my mind: This is my life now. Joey would never again be meeting me for dinner. John was there waiting for me instead, and there was nothing I could do about it. I could go home and stare at the ceiling and cry, or I could go in. I took a breath and walked through the door.

John saw me and smiled. He came over and kissed me on my cheek. Then he handed me a book, as a gift, that had meant a lot to him. He knew the author, who had written me a note on the first page. It was a thoughtful gift, and I was touched by the gesture. He thought that I would appreciate its words, and even though I was touched, I felt sick to my stomach. I hated that I was waiting in a crowded restaurant with a man I hardly knew. I wanted to run away. Sensing my unease, he suggested I have a glass of wine. I did not often drink, but I decided to have one to calm my nerves. It only took half a glass for me to relax and to enjoy his company and the attention he gave me. He told me I looked beautiful. I hardly felt beautiful; I was exhausted from grief and from caring for Sal and Vincent, but still, it sounded good.

I had two glasses of wine in total and that, along with dinner, put me in a very relaxed state. After dinner we went to a bar that had a live band. The music was great and I was actually having a good time, and that's when he asked if he could kiss me. In a fog from the wine and not really one hundred percent there, I answered yes. I remember feeling like a woman, and a part of me felt alive again. But I did feel guilty that he wasn't Joey.

We started dating. We were together a while before we had sex, and like the first kiss, wine was involved. I was still not over Joey and physically I still wanted him. But a couple of glasses helped me make the transition to John. I had been so used to Joey's anatomy. The first time I was with John, I could hear Joey's joke to me, "I ruined you for any other man." Of course he had been referring to his size, but he knew how much I loved him.

John and I had sex, and it was good, but I did not have the same connection to him that I did with Joey. I was not in love. This did not even bother me. I accepted that my life would never be the way it was before. I was comfortable being with a man I was not head-over-heels for. I was creating a new life that not only did not look like the old one, but did not feel like it either. With John I would never find myself crying on the basement floor. I was comforted by the fact that I would never feel that kind of pain again. It was enough for me that we were compatible.

We enjoyed the same things—going to the theater and to concerts, hearing live music. We could distract each other from the past. We had sex constantly as if it were a drug that could numb the pain in our hearts and make us feel alive again. The first few months together we spent a lot of time in bed. It was as if I were making up for the year and half of sexual drought since Joey's death. And for John, it was some sort of validation that he was still a man, because his failed marriage had made him feel like less than one. We were two wounded souls looking to escape, and for a while we did.

John had a lot of experience with things that I had never dealt with, and he was eager to help me. Joey had started renovating our house. I wanted to see his dream completed and around the time I started dating John, I started making plans to renovate. I had trouble finding an honest contractor though. John, being a real estate agent, knew one who was reliable and reasonable with costs. I hired him with John's help. In preparation for the renovation, the boys and I had already moved out of our house—to an apartment two houses away that I was renting from neighbors. It was an odd time of transience, renovating a house in Belle Harbor that Joey and I had called home, living in a rented apartment, and dreaming of a home in Manhattan.

John told me that sometimes listings in Manhattan could be reasonable, but they were rare. One night at dinner, he told me a story of a client who bought a townhouse for next to nothing. He could not believe the deal he had made, and he said it was like finding a needle in a haystack. "Keep your eyes open for another needle," I responded. I prayed that I would be as lucky, and a few months later John found a large, two-bedroom co-op apartment in Sutton Place, on the east side of Manhattan. The asking price was half the market price at that time, and even with the necessary renovations, it would be within my budget. I did not hesitate to buy it, and the contractor helping in Belle Harbor, agreed to do the work in Manhattan.

Our impending move to Manhattan opened up a new horizon for us. The boys and I would be able to walk or take a quick ride to all the places we loved. We would have a world of culture and diversity at our feet, but most importantly, I would be able to create a new life for us there.

The Second Anniversary of 9/11

I FIRST NOTICED THE SHIFT IN MY EMOTIONS ABOUT A MONTH after the first anniversary of Joey's death. I grew very angry with him for dying. My grief morphed into rage that he had put strangers' lives in front of his own family. How could he do that? How could he risk his own life to save others?

When I thought about the story the elevator mechanic had told me, I was livid. Joey knew that he could die, but he stayed there and did not run out. Why was he not thinking of his sons or of me? I fumed!

I told only my therapist about this. I could hardly say it out loud: "I'm angry at my hero husband." I felt guilty about my new reaction because I could see that sacrificing his life was a beautiful act and that not many people could do that. But in giving up his life for strangers, he left a gap in ours, one that could never be filled by anyone else. I would talk to him sometimes and say: "How could you do this to us? How could you help strangers?" I did not walk around angry all of the time, but it was definitely a new emotion.

When the second anniversary of Joey's death arrived, I had been dating John for about six months. He asked if I wanted to go out to dinner that night. I agreed to go and we had a nice dinner. I talked a lot about Joey. After dinner we decided to go to John's apartment for a quiet evening. It was empty at his apartment building. We were the only people in the lobby, the only two on the elevator. As the doors closed and it started to go up, it made a strange noise, bounced, and stopped. We were between floors and John flew into a panic. He pounded on the doors. He yelled for help. To say he didn't handle the situation calmly is an understatement. I was not as upset as he was and honestly felt we would be okay. As he freaked out, I could not help comparing him to Joey. Joey was calm and in control, especially during a crisis. It's what had made him a good firefighter, as well as someone I always felt safe with. This man was going crazy. Not only that, but he was so out of control I felt sure he could trample me in his haste to escape when we were rescued.

Watching him unravel made my understanding crystalize about why he could never take Joey's place in my heart. He was not a strong man—and yet, who was I to judge? I was not a strong woman. I would rather spend time with him than be alone. I would rather lie to myself and tell myself that he was right for me when I knew he wasn't. He lacked the character traits that I loved about men like Joey. Watching him act like a lunatic pounding on the door, I saw that he acted less like a man and more like a boy.

In between his ranting, we were able to hear the superintendent of the building shouting to us that he knew we were trapped and that it would only be a matter of time until we would be free. I decided to sit down and wait. I tried to get John to relax and join me on the floor, but he refused and continued to yell and pound. As I watched his theatrics, I smiled at the irony of this ridiculous situation. What were the chances of getting stuck in an elevator—and on of all days? It was crazy! I wondered if Joey had a hand in what was happening.

As the minutes dragged on, I did start to feel vulnerable. The elevator was not bouncing or falling. I was not afraid that anything bad would happen, but I did want to get out. How long would it take?

After about a half hour, I heard male voices on the outside and saw a Halligan tool—I knew the name because I'd quizzed Joey as he prepared for his exam. Of course they were firefighters coming to our rescue! I laughed to myself. If Joey wanted to get my attention, he had it. Being trapped on the second anniversary of 9/11 and being rescued by the FDNY was the way to go. I was no longer angry with him for saving strangers. I was now in the same position as the people he had saved that day: I needed help to get to safety, and I was being led there by firefighters who were just doing their job, just as Joey had done his, exactly two years earlier.

What would we have done without them? I was grateful they lived up to the pledge that they made—to go toward the chaos rather than run from it. I now understood fully how it felt to be in danger and powerless to solve the problem, and also how it felt to be rescued.

It was a gift I felt Joey gave me that night. I could finally understand why he stood firm in the lobby of the Marriott World Trade Center Hotel, and I loved him even more in that instant for being a man who lived by his word. I was proud of the man he had been and grateful for every moment we'd had together.

Joey was there that night. I felt strongly that in addition to letting me know why he had sacrificed his life, he was telling me he did not want me to waste mine. He wanted me to see John's true character.

From the beginning of our relationship, I had seen that John did not want to be a part of the boys' lives or act in any way like a father to them. He was nice to them when he saw them, but he did not see them often. I had not been happy about it, but I had convinced myself it had not mattered. I told myself I was happier with John in my life, that I was a better mother because of it. I rationalized that the boys benefited from him indirectly. The fact that I was not crying every minute was good for them. I had more energy to deal with them. I had companionship, which balanced my life, so I was a more balanced mother. At least that's what I told myself, but I knew it was lie. The truth was I just did not want to be alone. I was afraid that the pain I had felt after Joey died would be waiting for me.

Back on the Path

THE BOYS AND I MOVED INTO OUR SUTTON PLACE APARTMENT in January 2004. I had applied to a private progressive school in the West Village and both boys were accepted. They would start in the fall of 2004. In the meantime, I enrolled them in a Montessori school a block from our apartment. On Saturdays I took them to their swimming lessons, which were now just a quick trip across town. I joined a gym which the boys had access to on Sundays, so we could swim together. We spent our weekends at the museums, the gym, and in Central Park. I felt secure to be in a building that had a doorman twenty-four hours a day, seven days a week. If the boys fell asleep in my car, I could carry one of them into the lobby while the doorman kept an eye on my car until I carried the other one. If I had any problems with anything in the apartment, I could call the superintendent or the maintenance man and they would fix it. It was easier to be a single mother in an apartment building than it had been in our house, and living there allowed me to go in a new direction.

When the boys started their new school in the fall of 2004, I started a new phase of my healing process. A friend of John's, who had also become a friend of mine, was a captain in the FDNY. He had worked on 9/11 and he had also carried the dead body of his cousin out of what was left of his cousin's house when the plane crashed in Belle Harbor. He had suffered from Post-Traumatic Stress Disorder (PTSD) after those events, and he told me about EMDR therapy. When he found out I was still not able to sleep through the night, he knew that I was still suffering from PTSD. Even as a nurse, I had not recognized it. I had experienced nightmares, which I knew were part of it, but I never would have attributed my lack of sleep to it. I had simply learned to live with both. He told me I didn't have to. He had undergone EMDR therapy, and it had changed his life, as well as the lives of other firefighters he knew. It turned out the therapist he had seen was a few blocks from the boys' school, and she agreed to treat me. Through EMDR, I was able to start sleeping through the night as well as work through all the feelings that I was dealing with, past and present.

Because I was open to exploring new methods for dealing with my pain, I was headed down a new path. I was walking through my pain head on, and I was starting to change. I was no longer the woman that I had been when I first met John. Something inside of me had shifted. This made John very uncomfortable. He wanted me to continue to be that other woman—to go out and have a few drinks and spend most of my time with him, but I no longer felt the need, as he did, to be out at a bar socializing.

Body Parts

IN THE SPRING OF 2005 I RECEIVED A PHONE CALL FROM THE medical examiner's office. They wanted me to fill out and sign a form they were sending. They wanted me to send it back as soon as possible. It was a form they had sent me countless times over the past four years. It pertained to body parts. It let them know if I wanted to be informed, in the event that any other parts of Joey's body were found. I told them that I never filled out the form, because Joey was found in one piece. I thought the form was sent bureaucratically to all victims' families. I didn't think it pertained to me. They said they needed to have a signed copy for their files. "I'll fill it out," I said. I didn't think about it after that.

The next day I was walking down Fifth Avenue. I was on my way to the boys' school for parent teacher conferences, and I received a phone call from my mother-in-law. She asked me if I had heard from the medical examiner. "How did you know they called me?"

"They called my house trying to find a phone number for you. So, Vinnie, what are you going to do about it?"

"I'm going to fill out the form."

"Vinnie, what are you going to do?"

"I'll fill out the form and send it back."

She sounded strange. It was like she did not believe me. She kept asking me the same thing over and over: "What are you going to do about it?" I did not change my answer. She was agitated, and I was tired of talking in circles. I wanted to hang up. When I told her that I had to go, she said, "Vinnie, what are you going to do about my son's left leg and hip?"

A chill shot through my body, and my heart raced. "What did you say?"

"Vinnie, what are you going to do about Joey's leg and hip?"

"He was intact. What are you talking about?"

"His leg and hip are at the medical examiner's office."

"They never told me about his leg and hip. They asked me to fill out a form." I couldn't breathe. "I have to go." I felt like I was floating away from myself. It was 9/11 all over again. A dozen thoughts jammed my mind. How could this be? I sat with his body. It looked intact. I hadn't felt it, but it was whole. I remember how it looked. I could see the head and the feet in the body bag. I never touched it, but it was there. The firefighters who carried him out of Ground Zero had said he was all there, still wearing his turnout coat. They saw his mustache. I started to cry. I had always felt he had gone peacefully and quickly, and now I was picturing him ripped apart, and I was horrified by the thought of him being in pain. I hailed a cab and cried harder. I couldn't stop myself or calm down. I have to be at the boys' parent teacher conferences. I have to stop crying. They can't know. I moved to the city for privacy. I have to compose myself. No one must know.

I was good at hiding my pain. Even when I was having a bad day, I walked around with a smile on my face.

I shook my head. I have to compose myself. I'll take the taxi to my car. I'll get tissues, calm down.

I called John and I told him what had happened. He would call his father, who had a connection at the medical examiner's office, to verify the information for me. I knew my mother-in-law would never lie about such a thing, but John wanted to make sure it was the truth. When I got to my car, it was parked in front of a firehouse just a block from the boys' school. Normally I parked the car in front of the school. For some reason that morning I'd had trouble finding a spot. There were no tissues in the car. I went in the firehouse garage, which was open. I asked a young firefighter if he had a tissue.

"Are you okay?"

"Not really. I just found out that my husband's left leg and hip were found." When I saw his face, I realized he needed more information. "He was killed on 9/11, and I thought his body was intact, but it wasn't. He was a firefighter." The man handed me a tissue and said he would be right back. In seconds a captain appeared with him. He led me to an office, where I sat down and tried to calm myself. I was crying again, and I told him about the conferences and that I did not want to be late. I was unaware of how ridiculous I sounded. He gave me a phone and told me that I should cancel the conferences.

After I phoned the school, I sat there and tried to process the information. All that kept going through my mind was that Joey was ripped apart and had to have felt pain, and I could not bear that reality. For four years, I'd had a peaceful vision of Joey's death. Now I had horrible visions, and I was sliding into the abyss. I prayed for help.

While I prayed silently, a man walked into the office. I noticed his white hat. Officers wear white hats. He introduced himself and told me he was a chief. There was something about him that put me at ease the minute he walked in the door, and then he told me something that changed my world. He had been at the World Trade Center on 9/11. He was a captain then. He and his men were buried alive when the buildings collapsed. They had been helping an older woman down the stairs when it happened. He described hearing an incredibly loud noise. He heard one of his men yell, "Here it comes!" and then the world got very quiet and he felt a sense of calmness and peace. It was like nothing he had ever felt before. He assured me that it happened instantly. Joey did not feel a thing.

I could tell that he was speaking the truth. He was not just trying to make me feel better. I was so grateful he had been rescued and that he had been at this firehouse where my car just happened to be parked. I knew Joey was here again, and that this was no coincidence.

I stopped crying and readied myself to pick up the boys. The chief thought it would be best, though, if I went to the FDNY counseling unit. It was a few blocks away. There was a car waiting to take me there. I agreed to go, and I met with a therapist. She told me I should understand I was in shock again, no different than how I had felt on 9/11, and that I should try to relax for the rest of the day and night and allow myself time to get my equilibrium back. It was good to have support, and I was grateful it was there, but it was listening to the chief that had made all the difference to me. I had an understanding deep in my gut that Joey had died in peace. He had not suffered, and I was grateful to God for that awareness. But there was something else that Joey wanted me to know.

When I had called John that day, I was looking for his support. I did not get it. Instead, more of his characteristics were shown. He had called the medical examiner's office and verified that Joey's body parts had shown up. After he called to tell me that, I did not hear from him the rest of the day. That evening he did not come to my apartment, and he had been living with me. He went instead to a bar. When he did get home, he was drunk, and he blamed me for the day's events. I had nothing to say to him. It was a ridiculous accusation. Being drunk, he continued his verbal assault. He was full of energy and anger. I asked him to get out of my home, but he would not leave. I went into my room and locked my door. Eventually he fell asleep on my couch.

Joey kept trying to show me what I needed to see, and I continued to ignore it, but this time my feelings for John changed.

Letting Go and Moving On

I HAD STARTED TAKING YOGA CLASSES AS A WAY TO RELAX and increase my flexibility. I thought it would be good for my body. In order to practice yoga, I had to focus on my breathing and on the poses. I had to concentrate and relax as I tried to balance and stretch in different positions. "Take a deep breath and let go," the instructor would say. I was hoping for a more flexible body, but as I continued to take the classes, I found that yoga was having more of an effect on my mind. After I would finish a class, my mind would become quiet and I was able to see things more clearly. I could see the truth, and the truth was that I was unhappy with John.

After Joey's body parts showed up, I knew for certain that John was the wrong man for me. I could no longer distract myself from this truth. By practicing yoga, the distractions cleared, and all I could see was the truth. Yet, even with that knowledge, I felt paralyzed to take action. I was no longer afraid of being alone, but I was afraid if I broke up with John, it would hurt the boys. John was living with us and even though his contact with the boys was limited, they enjoyed his attention. I worried about Sal the most. I remembered how he had wept in my arms when he lost his father, and I was afraid of how he would deal with another loss. I also did not want to hurt John. He was not a bad person. He had helped me a great deal, and I cared about him. I was unsure of what to do.

We would be better off apart, but I had to figure out how to get there with the least amount of pain to all. I did tell John more than once that I thought he had a drinking problem and that he should get help. I would give him my support if he went for help, but he denied having a problem. On numerous occasions I told him that we were not right for each other and that I did not see a future for us. I was laying the groundwork for a break-up. I was hoping he would see for himself that it was not working and that he would want to leave.

At this time, I had made another big decision. I had put my house in Belle Harbor on the market. I could not afford to have two homes. I could have kept both if I had gone back to work, but that would have meant time away from the boys, and I was not willing to choose the house over them, so it was an easy choice. I now had a good reason to let go of the old life.

The renovated house was big and beautiful, but it was all smoke and mirrors without Joey. Even though it stood solid on its foundation, the life that had been lived within it had been washed away. This new house did not even resemble the old one. The only physical remnant from our old home was the frame that Joey had made with our house numbers, 169, the numbers that always made me smile when I thought of his rhyme. I could still hear his voice and his joke to me when we were not sleeping through the night because we were knee-deep in midnight feedings, diaper changes, and walking the dogs: "We're doing time at 169." That sweet sentence we were serving together, I would gladly take back, but our time there was over, and it was time to move on.

I felt a sense of freedom when I made my decision. It was just a house. The memories created there did not reside in its walls or foundation. They were in my heart, and they would always be there.

John was still living in my apartment, but our relationship was unraveling. It happened naturally. We were not spending time together. He was just sleeping in my bed. Eventually, I got the courage to break up officially. He was not happy about it, but he was more upset about not having a place to live. He had rented out his apartment a few months before and had given the renter a one-year lease, so he had no place to go. We were able to be friends, and I let him sleep on the couch and take his time finding a place. It did not feel right throwing him out. We remained friends. He was even helping me sell my house.

The first month the house was on the market, I had a buyer. John handled the contract with his friend, who was a lawyer. It should have been easy, because the buyer was paying cash, but it turned out that the architect had failed to file a certificate of occupancy with the city. Even though I had a contract for the sale of the house legally, I could not sell it without the certificate. Getting the certificate required a lot of time and effort. John was helping me, but it was a stressful situation, and he did not handle stress well. In the evenings he got drunk and angry. I had no tolerance for his behavior. He had to go. When I finally obtained the certificate and sold the house, I gave John some money and told him to leave. I felt bad kicking him out, but I had to put the wellbeing of the boys and myself ahead of him.

The whole time I was trying to obtain the certificate, I continued to practice yoga. It kept me calm and centered. Through all the chaos, I was able to see things clearly. Yoga gave me the power to see within myself. When I got quiet and followed my heart, I was able to stay on course and do the right thing for all of us, no matter how hard it was.

When I finally put our welfare ahead of John's, I gained a sense of balance, literally. There had been one pose that I'd had trouble with. It required me to balance on one leg. I could balance on one side, but never on the other. The day after I made John move out, I took a yoga class. As I attempted to balance on the side that always gave me trouble, something amazing happened. With hardly any effort, I was able to do it. I had struggled for so long and now it came to me so easily, like I had always been able to do it.

A New Life

With john gone, the energy in our home changed.
I went from feeling like I had to tip toe through life to a feeling
of peace and tranquility. I had worried that the boys would be sad
when John was gone, but it was quite the opposite. They seemed to
feel a sense of relief. They were happier, and with John gone I did
not have to put them to bed so early—on a couple of occasions they
had witnessed his temper, and to prevent it from happening again,
I had taken to putting them to bed by seven, well before the time
John came home. I remember Vincent at four years old saying to
me, "Why don't you get a new friend?" Now with their bedtime
later, we enjoyed each other's company longer. John was no longer
interrupting me when I read their bedtime stories. I was relieved
not to hear him knock loudly on their bedroom door saying, "It's
my time now."

I felt like we had all been emancipated. We enjoyed having
the freedom to live, which was sometimes messy. John could not
relax unless everything was in its place. I enjoyed the fact that I no
longer had to worry about him walking in and robotically putting
everything in order. It was not until he was gone that I realized how
compromised our life had become with him there.

I recovered my passion for cooking, too, and I shared it now with the boys. Before Joey died, I had always included Sal when I cooked. He would stand on the chair next to me. When he was two and a half, his favorite thing to make was pizza. We made the dough from scratch together. He liked to check the dough to see when it rose. Now Vincent and Sal would both help me prepare dinner. I taught the boys how to peel garlic and chop it, as well as sauté it. They made sauce with me, and when I made their favorite dish, chicken cutlets, we all had our hands in it, literally. We cracked and beat the eggs, dipped the chicken in the egg, grated the cheese, and then we breaded them in a mixture of plain bread crumbs, pecorino Romano cheese, parsley, garlic powder, and sea salt. The boys' hands resembled gloves made of a gooey, clumpy egg, cheese, and bread crumbs. Taking turns, we placed the cutlets with a fork in the pan, watched them brown, and turned them until they were crispy. It felt good to be cooking again.

The living room now became a place that we could actually live in. Some days it was covered by wooden railroad tracks and trains. Other times we would make a tent out of pillows and blankets and have a clubhouse. It was a wonderful mess, and I was a different mother to them now. I was relaxed and I had more confidence as a single parent. It had been four and a half years since Joey's death, and I was no longer afraid to raise the boys alone. I had been doing it alone all along anyway, even when John was there. I took the boys on vacations by myself, cared for them through illnesses, helped them with schoolwork, taught them right from wrong, showed them how to be compassionate and giving. They were growing into wonderful people, and I was resembling more and more the mother they had known before 9/11. I felt the sense of excitement and joy for them that I had when Joey was alive. I felt eager to share with them the things in life that I loved. One of those things was movies.

After spending a Saturday afternoon in Central Park, we came home, had dinner, and then I put on a movie I was sure they would enjoy. It was one of my favorites, and I could not wait to share it with them. The boys and I had been to the bookstore that morning. I had seen the DVD on the shelf, and I had grabbed it enthusiastically. The last time I had seen the movie was when I was dating Joey. It had been around Easter and one of the major networks was airing it. I told him it was one of my favorite movies and I asked him to watch it with me. He agreed, but I knew that he was only doing it for me. I was sure it was not a movie he would watch on his own. I was hoping he would enjoy it, though. As it played, I could see that he didn't hate it. Whether it was the truth or a lie, he said that he liked it.

That night after I cleaned the dishes, the boys and I got into our PJs. We popped some popcorn. I melted butter, and we poured it over the kernels, then salted it. The aroma of fresh popcorn filled the apartment. We snuggled up under a big fuzzy blanket together. I was in the middle with Sal on my right and Vincent on my left. I had the large bowl of popcorn on my lap. We took handfuls of popcorn. I pressed the remote control to start, and then I waited.

On the screen there were mountains, then clouds, then the sound of wind. The boys and I watched as more images appeared—hillsides, a river. We heard the different instruments begin to play, softly at first. Aerial shots of castles, pine trees, and then there she was, walking with her arms spread wide spinning in an open meadow as she sang: "The hills are alive, with the sound of music . . ."

After Julie Andrews sang, and the overture played, the kids giggled as I sang and danced around the living room, the music so beautiful and familiar. Then I snuggled in again and the boys and I sat back as we became part of that world. The boys never lost interest. During the intermission we took a little break, and I gave them some ice cream. They were excited for the movie to start when the intermission ended. They were enjoying it, and I was thrilled. Seeing the movie with them was like watching it for the first time, but I had a different understanding of the movie watching it now. I related to the captain completely. He kept away from anything that reminded him of his wife, who had died. I had been doing the same thing. I had tried to protect myself by living a life that did not resemble my old one. In my effort not to get hurt, I was not really living. I could see that now so clearly.

As the boys and I watched the movie, we sang along to the songs. I felt a sense of optimism and renewal. I was grateful that they were still young and that I had time to spend with them.

I loved that *The Sound of Music* was based on real events. If the captain could find love again, then maybe someday I could, too. I was happy that someone had taken the time to write about Captain von Trapp, his children, and Maria. Their story gave me inspiration and hope, and seeing it on screen made me consider my own life story. Maybe someday I would write it.

For now, I had no other plans. I sat between Sal and Vincent, my heart bursting with love and gratitude. As the movie ended and they climbed the mountain to freedom, I thought about the many mountains ahead for us to climb, but we would do it together. I had confidence that, God willing, I would be able to hold their hands along the way.

MARCH 2006

Epilogue

THE BOYS AND I LIVE HAPPILY IN NEW YORK CITY. THEY ARE both teenagers now, taller than me and growing into kind and compassionate men. We have two dogs, smaller in size than Chelsea and Durante, but big in heart and just as dear. We remain friends with Joan, Kelly, Mike and Denise, and our neighbors from Belle Harbor. Joan works nearby, and we often see her. And Kelly, once the boys' babysitter, has grown into a beautiful, intelligent woman. And through Divine guidance, I'm in love with a wonderful family man, father of three children. Today, we are a party of seven, and it's far more entertaining than *The Brady Bunch*.

We are blessed.

Acknowledgments

All of my love and gratitude go to my boys, Sal and Vincent, for their encouragement and for the inspiration they provided me. I send love and gratitude also to my mother and brother for their belief in me and for their generosity in allowing me to be truthful. I want to thank my mother, specifically, for her incredible sense of humor, intuition, and love. To my in-laws, I remain forever grateful for the gift of your son. Last but not least, I thank Kelly for her wisdom, honesty, and friendship. You were amazing with the boys.

I am thankful for the feedback and support from Mary, Lori, Cassandra, Rosalie, Vanessa and Mike, Annette, and Clodagh who read the first drafts. Your encouragement and advice made all the difference.

I will be forever grateful to Lisa Dale Norton whose literary excellence and intuitive understanding shaped and crafted my drafts into a cohesive story. I thank God that I picked up her book *Shimmering Images*. Her proficiency shines through every page.

I thank Melissa Rosati for her expertise in publishing as well as coaching. Melissa, you provided me with a compass so that I could make my way through the publishing process. Your knowledge and insight are appreciated. I am also grateful to Betsy Robinson for her editorial help. I also want to thank Gerald and Sheila Levine at Levine Samuel, LLP for their advice and support.

And, all of my love to you, Jarrett, for your patience, love, and support. Love is vast, infinite, and unconditional.

On September 11, 2001, and the days and months that followed, I saw the very best in humanity. The love, compassion, and support that people from the United States and around the world so freely shared overwhelmed me. I was able to understand that in spite of the attacks, the world we share has far more love than evil.

Thank you to my family and close friends, I appreciate all the love and support that you gave to the boys and me. Special thanks to Joey's cousins; I appreciate your generosity. And to my cousin Nicky, thanks for your time and support.

I will always be grateful for the outpouring of support given to me by the Rockaway community. The list of people and businesses could fill pages. Special thanks to Dr. Terrence Mundy, DC, and Dr. Nancy Ghales, DC, Dr. Locke, and Leslie. I felt your support when I needed it the most. My heartfelt gratitude goes to my neighbors for their generosity, care, and assistance. Thank you, Kas, Joan and Steven, Joanne and Mike, Mary and Tom, Debbie and Steve, Kelly and Lorraine, Denise and Mike, Kevin and Sally, Susan and Billy, Gerry and John and Claire, and so many others. You all bravely walked into our lives and gave freely of your time and energy. Your compassion and support made all the difference to us.

Special thanks to the Belle Harbor neighbor, who enabled the families from the State of Washington to send care packages to the boys and me every month. To the Washington families: We will always be grateful to you. We loved opening the boxes and receiving the artwork, gifts, and goodies that your families so generously gave.

Thank you to the doctors and staff at Long Island Pediatrics for your kindness, generosity, and support.

Thanks to my fellow nurses and staff members who were always available to speak with me by phone, day and night in those first weeks after 9/11. When I was not sleeping, I knew one of you would be there to answer the phone. Your prayers and support will never be forgotten.

My deepest gratitude goes to Suze Orman, Kathy, and Carol who gave freely of their time and energy. I also thank Nancy Carbone.

Thank you to the kind and generous people from all over America who sent Teddy Bears, quilts, jewelry, artwork, cards, and letters. It was very much appreciated. Thank you to the FDNY Family Assistance Unit for getting it to us and for all of your continued support.

Thank you to the Brooklyn Heights neighbors of Engine 205 and Ladder 118 for all of your generosity and thoughtfulness.

Thank you to the UFA and UFOA for all of your assistance then and now.

A special heartfelt thanks to our family of brave men at Engine 205 and Ladder 118. The care and support given to the boys and me will never be forgotten. Your efforts in the rescue and recovery of your brothers, as well as the care given to their families, went so far above and beyond the call of duty. All of you are heroes.

A final word of thanks to first responders everywhere for putting your lives on the line everyday.

Book Group Discussion Guide

When we come together to read books and share stories, we learn from each other and strengthen our communities. Organized by categories, these questions serve as prompts for group discussions. If your group would like to ask VinnieCarla questions or to include her in your discussion via phone, Skype, or Google Hangouts, please contact media@amorepress.com.

GENERAL QUESTIONS

1. Where were you on 9/11?
2. What do you find to be the most interesting topics in the book and why?
3. Which section of the book was the most emotional to read? Why?
4. Describe VinnieCarla's strengths and weaknesses as a mother?
5. How does money affect relationships?
6. What impact did victim compensation payouts to families have on relationships in the community?
7. What role does gossip play throughout the book?
8. After reading this book, what are you personally inspired to do differently in your daily life?

QUESTIONS ABOUT LOSS

1. How did VinnieCarla's experiences with her parents prepare her (or not) for dealing with the trauma of losing Joey?

2. As a parent, have you had an experience where you felt you could not protect your child?

3. What do you think about the way VinnieCarla talked to Sal about his father?

4. What do you think about VinnieCarla's decision not to show emotion at the funeral?

5. VinnieCarla's grief and sexual desire are intertwined. How well does she navigate the social taboos?

6. How did VinnieCarla's decision to euthanize Durante change her understanding of grief?

QUESTIONS ABOUT LOVE

1. What details of VinnieCarla's story about meeting Joey are similar to your first meeting with someone you are (or were) involved with in a romantic relationship?

2. What did Joey's death teach VinnieCarla about love?

3. Are there aspects of this memoir that feel like a love letter to Joey? Identify the passages.

QUESTIONS ABOUT INTUITION

4. What part of VinnieCarla's dream experiences were most illuminating for you?

5. Do you think it was pure coincidence that VinnieCarla and John were stuck in the elevator on the second anniversay of 9/11?

6. Throughout the book, VinnieCarla's intuition appears strongest in life-threatening situations. Which situation intrigues you the most?

QUESTIONS ABOUT HEALING

1. How has the book changed or enhanced your view of mental health issues?

2. In what ways was VinnieCarla's connection to the Virgin Mary healing?

3. How does VinnieCarla manage to walk the emotional tightrope with her mother and her in-laws? How is her strategy similar or different to your relationship tightropes?

4. What did you think about VinnieCarla's decision to contact Suze Orman?

5. VinnieCarla takes her children to Disney several times. With each visit, what healing occurs for her?

QUESTIONS ABOUT SPIRITUALITY AND FAITH

1. Have you ever felt the energetic presence of loved ones around you?

2. Where does VinnieCarla blur the lines between praying versus bargaining with God?

3. How does VinnieCarla's relationship with God change throughout the book?

4. In the "Ghost" section, do you believe that Vincent really saw his father?

5. Throughout the book, VinnieCarla believes Joey's presence is with her. Do you believe this is true? Why or why not? How is her belief healing?

QUESTIONS ABOUT THE WRITER'S CRAFT

1. Describe VinnieCarla's sense of humor.

2. VinnieCarla reveals intimate details about her feelings. Are there sections in her story where you felt it was too much information? Were there sections where you wanted more?

3. Characterize VinnieCarla's writing style. What makes her voice unique?

4. How does VinnieCarla use popular culture references to anchor her narrative? From these references, what are your strongest associations?

5. Compare and contrast this book with other memoirs you've read about loss and recovery.